Also by Anna Pump and Gen LeRoy

Country Weekend Entertaining
The Loaves and Fishes Cookbook

Summer on a Plate

More than 120 Delicious,

No-Fuss Recipes for

Memorable Meals from

Loaves and Fishes

ANNA PUMP AND GEN LeROY

Photography by Alan Richardson

Simon & Schuster
New York   London   Toronto   Sydney

Simon & Schuster
1230 Avenue of the Americas
New York, NY 10020

First Simon & Schuster hardcover edition June 2008

SIMON & SCHUSTER and colophon are registered trademarks of Simon & Schuster, Inc.

For information about special discounts for bulk purchases,
please contact Simon & Schuster Special Sales at
1-800-456-6798 or business@simonandschuster.com.

Designed by Nancy Singer

Manufactured in the United States of America

10 9 8 7 6 5 4 3 2 1

Library of Congress Cataloging-in-Publication Data
Pump, Anna.
    Summer on a plate : more than 120 delicious, no-fuss recipes for memorable meals from
Loaves and Fishes / Anna Pump and Gen LeRoy ; photography by Alan Richardson.
p. cm.
    1. Loaves and Fishes (Store : Sagaponack, N.Y.)
    2. Cookery. 3. LeRoy, Gen. I. Title.

TX652.P92 2008
641.5 dc—22
2007048932

ISBN-13: 978-1-4165-4285-8
ISBN-10:   1-4165-4285-X

For Detlef

Acknowledgments

First and foremost I wish to thank Gen. Without her, there would be no book.

I want to thank my husband, Detlef, whose support, hearty appetite, and encouragement never stopped.

I could not have done this without Sybille van Kempen, my daughter, who is always there with new ideas and who, during the busy summer months, keeps Loaves and Fishes on track. I would also like to thank the entire staff at Loaves and Fishes for their hard work and their unwavering commitment to quality and freshness.

A special thanks to all my loyal customers who, summer after summer, with their praise and gentle critiques, inspire me to come up with new and challenging ideas.

Thanks to our superb editor, Sydny Miner, my agent and friend, Alison Bond, the excellent creative team at Simon & Schuster, Alan Richardson, Jackie Seow, and Michael Pederson, and a special thanks to Alice Mayhew for believing in me.

Finally, a big hug and thanks to all my family for sharing my food while testing and retesting all the recipes and offering their honest critiques—nothing "sugar-coated" as my grandchildren would call it.

—A. P.

Contents

Why This Book?

*I*t was during one evening last summer, when my friend Alison and I were dining at the Dockside restaurant in Sag Harbor, overlooking the bay with dozens of gleaming boats anchored only a few feet away, that the idea for this book was born. I had been chattering almost nonstop about all the new combinations of tastes and blendings of textures I wanted to try, also about nurturing some newer, fun recipes, about ideas for quick and easy meals, when Alison leaned over and said with a knowing smile, "You're going to write another book, Anna, aren't you?" I couldn't help but smile. Of course! I even had a title ready—*Summer on a Plate*. It had been in the back of my mind for quite a while and now, speaking openly about it, a summer cookbook seemed like the most natural and, to me, most obvious way to offer recipes that I had accumulated over the years, the majority of which were designed especially for the summer season when Loaves and Fishes is open full time.

I wanted to create a cookbook that celebrated summer's glorious bounty from the fields, farms, gardens, and seas. I wanted it to be a book for those of us who adore summertime and summer food and would like to pick up some handy shortcuts for preparing quick, tasty meals in an hour or less from start to finish.

Life should become easier during the summer, when afternoons grow longer and we are able to find peaceful times to lunch on a blanket stretched under a tree, or lie in a hammock while nursing a tall drink, or spend an afternoon picnicking at the beach, or relish those lengthy dusk-to-dark evenings when each sunset is more spectacular than the last. Which brings us to the core of this book: designing easy-to-read, no-fuss, delicious, and memorable meals that will still allow the cook time to enjoy all the pleasures that our summer season has to offer.

Trends in food come and go. People want new ideas, and as soon as any appear they seem to be instantly embraced by anyone who owns a pan. That, to me, is the fun part of creating new recipes; the one thing that has always remained constant is my absolute commitment to good food. I shop and strongly recommend shopping for the finest, top-quality ingredients: my conviction is that all of us should be able to enjoy every kind of food in moderation. It is the principle that lies at the heart of Loaves and Fishes.

Each and every spring, I cannot wait to hang the "Welcome" sign out front of the store, fling open the windows, give the picnic table in back a good scrubbing, and arrange the table in my garden at home in such a way as to catch the dappled sunshine that filters down through the leaves during the day and allows us the fullest view of those moonlit, starry skies at dinner time.

In this book I want to share with you the joy, the thrill of summer cooking. I want to encourage every home cook to take risks, adapt, add to, or subtract from these recipes that are, after all, blueprints for meals that can turn the modest cook into an instant star. That, to me, is the hope behind this book: that you enjoy the recipes as much as I have loved creating them in my heartfelt salute to summer.

How It All Began

It's been twenty-five years since that fateful day when, having heard there was a small cooking store for sale in Sagaponack, Long Island, I drove over and looked it over carefully. A soft natural light spilled in from the bank of windows in front and on one side of the main room, which made the room appear larger than it was. I walked behind the wooden counter and into the kitchen, which seemed to be just the right proportions for someone like me who had catered parties for years, mostly from my own country kitchen in Noyac, sometimes using my customers' kitchens, and many times on outdoor grills under vast tents. The store—already called Loaves and Fishes—was cozy, and I was able to see that its size was certainly manageable. Its embracing atmosphere made me feel immediately at home, and after spending more time inside and then outside in the small, charming garden I decided that I had to buy it.

My husband, Detlef, and I scrubbed the inside from top to bottom, repainted everything white, even the floors, made sure all the facilities were in A-1 condition, weeded the back garden, and planted herbs and vegetables. As we worked, I allowed my imagination to run rampant; new recipes began cluttering my brain, ideas that I had been yearning to test and try but had no space in which to develop were now in almost my every thought. I was, at the same time, excited and terrified. Time flew by at an alarming rate. The season was to begin in approximately two weeks from the time Detlef and I finally mopped our way out the back door. I began buying, storing, planning, baking—I felt as if I had suddenly sprouted eight arms, all of them moving simultaneously. Suddenly, it seemed, opening day was upon us. I had not stopped, filling the shelves with my own freshly baked breads, scones, muffins, pies, and cakes; the cookie jars were gradually filling to their brims, each food bin held new and, I hoped, innovative salads, meats, pastas, grains, and vegetables. Ducks and chickens, crisp and still steaming, were slid off the spits and lined up on a huge wooden tray. Room was made for the savory tarts and the whole roasts, sliced, garnished, and ready to go. Pâtés, dips, dressings, sauces, and hors d'oeuvres were placed in my brand-new freezer and I can't even remember what else, but, believe me, there was more, much more.

When our doors opened, I had been there since before 4:00 a.m., the time when our ovens needed to be turned on for the day's baking. I slipped on a clean and starched white jacket and opened the front door. The shock on my face must have been quite apparent because the first few customers in the line that stretched to the road and curled up its side smiled back at me, and some laughed at my surprised expression. I welcomed everyone inside, and within a few short hours I was putting more ducks and chickens on the spits, whipping up more salads, and taking orders for parties of ten to forty. At around 4:00 p.m. I sat down and treated myself to a cup of strong coffee and a cookie. I felt a glow of extreme pleasure. It had become apparent that this was possibly the beginning of the most exciting, challenging, and demanding part of my life. Looking back at it with today's perspective, it was. And still is.

Summer, for me, begins when the first signs of spring appear, when the earth is launched on its gradual thaw and we can almost sense life beginning to unfold beneath our feet. Windows stay open and breezes begin to usher in intoxicating aromas. Honeybees begin circling fresh flowers or plants that have blossomed overnight. Rows of seedlings in the garden behind Loaves and Fishes begin their greening, and as far as the eye can see, all along the village streets and country roads, plumpish buds are ready to dazzle us with their gorgeous palettes.

It's when April arrives that I begin my early morning ritual of bicycling to the beach. The air is crystal clear, crisp and incredibly invigorating. As I pedal down the hilly road to Main Beach, I pass the seafood shop where our local fishermen, still in their hip-high rubber boots, are delivering crates filled with their catches of the day; seagulls are swirling overhead. I immediately imagine recipes dealing with fish, shrimp, scallops, lobster. I make a mental note to check out what is the freshest and when to expect a delivery to the store.

The air is beginning to warm up as I eventually reach town where the vintage homes are being dressed up for the season; new paint, new cedar shingles, new roofs, flower boxes with baby buds peeking over the rims, trees being pruned, lawns resodded, and behind one house, I can see a young woman scrubbing her grill on the back patio.

I love summer.

Farmers have plowed their fields, potatoes and corn are planted. Outdoor farm stands have begun to display freshly picked young vegetables: baby peas, beans, spinach, white eggplants, greens of all sorts, and baskets overflowing with zucchini, their large, drooping flowers hanging over the edges. What will my customers, many of whom have become close friends over the years, like me to suggest they buy? How should it be prepared? Questions like what reheats well? What is best served chilled? Which foods are safe to bring to the beach? How long does this or that salad, meat, cheese, or vegetable last—these are ones I answer many times each day.

I am delighted to discover fresh goat cheese on sale, local and divine. Green strawberry fields are dotted in red. Hand-painted signs that invite anyone to PICK YOUR OWN remind me of a time, not long ago, when we brought our grandchildren to these annual rituals; their fingers, shirts, and mouths would be stained pink at the end of our outings.

I love preparing food in summer because it's when the freshest produce is so easily accessible and cooking options become limitless. It is my season. The best time to spread my wings, be creative, be inspired, be challenged and like those buds in our flower boxes, I actually feel blessed by the sun and raring to blossom.

Summer on a Plate

Keeping a Step Ahead

What to Buy, How to Store It, What to Freeze

The first rule for preparing no-fuss meals is to have everything you need on hand before you start. All the essential ingredients should be properly stored in your pantry, refrigerator, or freezer. Let's tackle the pantry first.

I know it seems silly to mention salt since it is a common staple used on or in almost everything we eat. I also know that consumer markets and magazines have been bombarded recently with salts of every description and color, harvested from almost every region in the world. For me, kosher salt is and has always been a particular favorite. It has a flakelike texture that allows it to dissolve more easily, has no additives, and with a slightly more pungent taste than ordinary table salt, a pinch goes a long way. Also, if you enjoy a little crunch in your salad that will awaken the taste buds, this is the salt to use.

I'm sure you've been told this many times, but a high-quality imported cold-pressed extra virgin olive oil with a deep, fruity body is a *must*. Safflower, peanut, walnut, canola, and toasted sesame oils should be on your shelves, as well as a bottle of soy sauce. Place a really good aged balsamic vinegar at the top of your list: use it in salad dressings, drizzled on fish, poultry, and in sauces that need a bit of vigor. Rice vinegar, white vinegar, red wine vinegar, and sherry vinegar are all essential to summer cooking and fortunately have very long shelf lives. Preground pepper loses its potency within three to four months, whereas whole peppercorns, stored in a cool, dry place, can last up to a year—the difference between freshly ground and preground pepper is enormous. Other pantry essentials are capers, sesame seeds, red pepper flakes, and mustards—Dijon, in particular. Here's a recipe for a most wonderful and resourceful piquant mustard sauce that you'll find yourself using over and over again.

Grainy Mustard Sauce

½ cup grainy mustard
½ cup Crème Fraîche (page 30)
2 tablespoons olive oil
1 tablespoon honey
¼ teaspoon kosher salt
¼ teaspoon cayenne pepper

Whisk all the ingredients in a bowl until smooth. Serve at room temperature.

Yields about 1 cup

❈ For chicken, add finely chopped fresh basil

❈ For lamb, add minced mint leaves

❈ For beef, add minced curly parsley or cilantro

Then there are brandy, framboise, and, of course, wines that need to be considered. The wines and alcohol I use in my cooking are ones that I could and would serve to my guests. Don't skimp on any of these items; the better the ingredient, the better your food.

Many recipes call for fresh herbs which, as a rule, are plentiful in the summer, yet I suggest you buy a small supply of dried herbs such as bay leaves, thyme, tarragon, rosemary, mint, dill, oregano, chives, and basil, in case the herbs you want are simply not available. Keep in mind that dried herbs shouldn't be kept for more than six months. Almost every herb can be preserved in oil, and infused oils flavored with individual herbs are an excellent addition to salad dressings, pasta sauces, etc. It's remarkable how quickly the oil absorbs each herb's unique flavor—when you open the bottle the scent is so wonderfully intense.

A tablespoon or two of rosemary oil is great in stews and soups. If you're making fish, try adding a splash of dill or thyme oil. Chive-infused oil is good on about anything raw or cooked. Basil and oregano oils add a gorgeous scent to pasta sauces, sautéed vegetables, and omelets. Depending on your individual tastes, the possibilities are enormous.

Herb-Infused Oil

    4 loosely packed cups fresh herbs, leaves only, washed and dried
    2 cups best-quality olive oil

Using a food processor, combine the ingredients and process until the herb is finely minced. Pour the infused oil into a plastic container with a lid. Cover and refrigerate for up to 3 months. Make sure each container is correctly labeled and dated.

Yields about 2½ cups

Fresh basil patches release the most magnificent aromas in summer. When the leaves are puréed with garlic and oil, its concentrated flavor allows a little of it to do its job well. We use our pesto, which is made without cheese, on pastas, in salads, to enrich the flavor of sauces, with fish, chicken—you name it. Here's an easy-as-pie pesto recipe we've been using for years, sometimes substituting walnuts for the pine nuts.

Pesto

¼ cup pine nuts
1½ tablespoons minced garlic
2½ cups tightly packed basil leaves
¾ cup olive oil
½ teaspoon kosher salt
½ teaspoon freshly ground black pepper

Process the pine nuts and garlic in a food processor for 30 seconds, until well combined. Add the basil, oil, salt, and pepper and purée until smooth.

Yields 1¼ cups

❉ Double or triple the ingredients and freeze in ice cube trays. When set, remove the pesto cubes from the trays and store in a resealable plastic bag. Use the individual cubes as additions to sauces, dips, or dressings. Or freeze in 1-cup plastic containers for larger needs. Frozen, it lasts forever. Covered and refrigerated, it lasts up to 3 months.

Buy the best quality spices: cinnamon, allspice, cloves, ground white pepper, cayenne pepper, sage, saffron, and curry powder. Really good curry is a creation of many spices, such as coriander, turmeric, fenugreek, cumin, cayenne pepper, ginger, allspice, and nutmeg. We mustn't forget the unique and costly saffron that is a requisite for many European and Middle Eastern dishes. Don't get powdered saffron—you never know if or how it's been adulterated. Best to buy a few threads of saffron that, when stored in an airtight container and kept in a cool dark place, will last up to six months. It's a colorful, pungent, aromatic spice that brightens all sorts of rice dishes, risottos, and, of course, bouillabaisse.

If you bake, almond extract is a good idea—and of course vanilla extract. Get the real thing; it may be more expensive but it's worth it. If you're making custards, chantilly cream, pie fillings, cakes, cookies, or almost any kind of pudding, the recipe will most likely require a teaspoon or so of vanilla. Here's a wonderful recipe that is so easy and lasts forever.

Vanilla Beans in Vodka

12 whole vanilla beans (I use Madagascar beans)

3 cups vodka

Stand the vanilla beans in a tall jar with a tight-fitting lid. Pour in enough vodka to entirely cover the beans. Put the lid in place and store at room temperature for three weeks, allowing the beans to soften. Use the liquid as you would any commercial extract; simply make sure the vanilla beans are always fully immersed in vodka.

> ≉ For a special flavor, remove a bean from the vodka, cut off the tip, and squeeze some essence into your recipe—your guests will notice the taste instantly. Return the same bean to the vodka and it will continue flavoring the extract.

Yields 3 cups

Keeping a step ahead can be as simple as adding mint leaves or slivers of lemon or lime to each compartment of your ice cube trays. After the ice is frozen, seal the cubes in plastic bags. It's a delightful way to dress up tall glasses of iced tea, seltzer water, or just about any mixed cocktail.

Toss some walnuts, pecans, almonds, pine nuts, and hazelnuts into your shopping cart; when you get home, seal them in plastic bags and freeze them. Nuts will last much longer when stored this way. Bread crumbs, too, ought to be sealed and stored in the freezer.

You will need raisins, shredded coconut, and dried cherries, all to be kept inside airtight containers. Don't forget that unbleached all-purpose flour, whole-wheat flour, panko bread crumbs, cornmeal, wild rice, couscous, wheat berries, and plain rice should also be stored inside airtight jars.

The use of salt in commercial butter is to preserve its shelf life. To control the amounts in our recipes, we only use unsalted butter. I love its taste and freshness. If you wish to use unsalted butter (and I do recommend it) and your intent is not to use it all within one week, then store it in your freezer, which is what I do.

Many recipes call for sautéing with clarified butter. Because it has no milk residue, clarified butter won't burn when cooked over high temperatures. Here's what you do:

Clarified Butter

Melt 16 tablespoons (8 ounces) unsalted butter over low heat. Do not allow it to boil. Skim the foam off the top. Pour the clear butter into a crock or clean jar, leaving any milky residue at the bottom of the pan to be discarded. Cover and refrigerate for up to 3 weeks.

Yields ¾ cup (12 tablespoons), but can easily be doubled

I suggest you make and freeze uncooked pie shells. When ready to use, unwrap the shell, fill it, and bake it. Once you've accomplished this easy task and reaped the benefits, you'll be making these pie shells throughout the year. This amazingly simple recipe can be used for dessert pies or savory tarts.

Pie or Tart Shells

> 4 cups unbleached all-purpose flour
> 12 tablespoons (6 ounces) cold unsalted butter, cut into small pieces
> 12 tablespoons (6 ounces) cold margarine, cut into small pieces
> ½ cup plus 2 tablespoons cold water

Place the flour, butter, and margarine in a food processor fitted with a metal blade. Pulse 5 or 6 times until the mixture becomes crumbly. With the motor running, add the water all at once and process until the dough starts to cling together. Turn the dough onto a lightly floured surface, gather it into a ball, flatten the ball into a disk, wrap it in plastic, and refrigerate the dough for 30 minutes.

Unwrap the dough and cut the disk into four equal pieces. Working on a lightly floured surface, roll out each piece into ⅛-inch-thick rounds. Fit each round into its own 9-inch pie dish or tart pan. Carefully wrap each shell in foil, label, and freeze.

When ready to use, discard the foil and assemble the tart or pie with your favorite filling. The crust will be much crisper when baked this way.

Yields 4 crusts

Starters

*I*f you think of a meal in musical terms, starters would be the overture, a prelude to the evening's style and ambiance. Starters can be exceptional, expensive, and exotic, passed around on silver trays, or can be as casual as a variety of dips arranged on a buffet or coffee table with bowls of crostini, raw vegetables, or toasted pita chips, to satisfy a variety of tastes. Starters sharpen the appetite for what lies ahead; therefore, it is important to plan the beginning of your gathering, plain or fancy, so as not to risk offering anything too filling, too rich, too much, too messy, or even too little. *Balance* is the key word here. What you're working toward is to serve a main course without taxing anyone's digestion or clouding the palate.

Presentation is another consideration since it helps to set the nature and spirit of the occasion. Almost all my outdoor meals are easy-going, relaxed, informal—so for those get-togethers, I browse through an enormous cache of wooden bowls and trays that Detlef and I have collected from various trips we've taken over the years. A particular favorite of mine happens to be a long grainy wooden board that shines up beautifully and looks marvelously inviting when it's blanketed with bite-size morsels grouped around an array of delicious dips and pâtés.

For more formal outdoor dinners, I reach onto a long shelf that lines our kitchen wall, close to the beamed ceiling, and carefully take down some very special pieces that belonged to my mother; gorgeous porcelain platters, china sauce boats, and pitchers. It was her love of cooking and gift for baking and entertaining that inspired me in the first place, so it has always seemed appropriate to have her represented at our candlelit table encircled by friends, strains of music in the background, great food, conversation, and laughter—in other words—everything wonderful!

Tomato–Avocado Salsa

This is a refreshing accent to grilled pork or chicken and a great dip with tortilla chips.

  1 avocado, peeled, pitted, and cut into ½-inch chunks

  1 teaspoon fresh lime juice

  3 tomatoes, peeled, seeded, and coarsely chopped

  ⅓ cup diced red onion

  1 clove garlic, minced

  1 small jalapeño pepper, seeded and minced

  ½ teaspoon ground cumin

  1 teaspoon kosher salt

  2 tablespoons olive oil

  1½ tablespoons red wine vinegar

  ¼ cup finely chopped fresh cilantro

Place all the ingredients in a medium bowl. Toss gently until well combined. Serve immediately.

  ❋ This salsa can be made a few hours ahead of time except for the avocados, which brown when left in the salsa. Add them when ready to serve.

Yields about 3 cups

Clam and Bacon Dip

Every time we make this dip it is consumed with amazing speed and gusto! At Loaves and Fishes we steam the clams in a little white wine and as soon as they open, we drain them, saving some liquid to use in the dip.

6 slices bacon

8 ounces cream cheese, softened

¼ cup mayonnaise

¼ cup sour cream

¼ teaspoon cayenne pepper

½ teaspoon kosher salt

12 ounces chopped cooked clams, drained

2 tablespoons clam juice

1 tablespoon minced curly parsley

½ cup chopped fresh chives, plus 1 tablespoon for garnish

Cook the bacon in a preheated 375°F oven for 30 minutes until crisp, or in a skillet on the stovetop. Let the bacon drain on paper towels until cool. Crumble and set it aside.

In a food processor or blender purée the cream cheese, mayonnaise, sour cream, cayenne, and salt for 30 seconds. Scrape the mixture into a bowl. Add the clams, clam juice, parsley, chives, and bacon pieces. Stir to blend well.

Serve the dip, garnished with the extra chives and thin slices of crusty French bread.

Yields about 2½ cups

* To save time, buy chopped clams from your seafood store or specialty food shop; they will work just fine.

* This dip can be made a day ahead, covered, refrigerated, and brought to room temperature before serving.

Roasted Tomato Dip

We center this rustic dip on a tray heaped with raw vegetables such as jicama, carrots, fennel, and peppers, cut into sturdy sticks. Or try this on toast or grilled bread.

> 6 small plum tomatoes, quartered
>
> 2 tablespoons olive oil
>
> 2 cloves garlic, split lengthwise
>
> 6 ounces cream cheese
>
> ¼ cup sour cream
>
> 1¼ teaspoons kosher salt
>
> 1½ teaspoons freshly ground black pepper
>
> 2 teaspoons chopped fresh chives, for garnish

Preheat the oven to 425°F.

Place the tomatoes, olive oil, and garlic in a small roasting pan. Toss to coat and roast for 25 minutes. Cool.

Transfer to a food processor and pulse 5 or 6 times. Add the cream cheese, sour cream, salt, and pepper and process until smooth. Garnish with chives before serving.

Yields 2½ cups

* If you make this ahead of time, let it stand at room temperature for 1 hour before serving.

* This dip can be made up to 2 days before, covered, and refrigerated, and again, brought to room temperature before serving.

Salmon Tartare with Honey Mustard on Whole-Grain Bread

This is a nice addition to any cocktail party, any season of the year. Mound the tartare in the center of a platter lined with mesclun greens and garnished with lime wedges and sprigs of dill. It is a beautiful presentation. On the side serve slices of whole-grain bread spread with honey mustard and let your guests help themselves.

1½ pounds fresh salmon fillet, skin and bones removed

½ cup finely chopped red onion

1 clove garlic, minced

1½ teaspoons kosher salt

1 teaspoon freshly ground black pepper

¼ cup capers, drained and coarsely chopped

3 tablespoons fresh lime juice

1 tablespoon olive oil

½ cup finely chopped fresh dill

Honey Mustard Spread

½ cup honey mustard

½ cup mayonnaise

½ teaspoon kosher salt

½ teaspoon freshly ground black pepper

8 slices whole-grain bread

Chop the salmon into ¼-inch chunks. Place the salmon pieces in a bowl with the onion, garlic, salt, pepper, capers, lime juice, olive oil, and dill and toss to combine it thoroughly. Cover and chill the tartare for at least 20 minutes or up to 24 hours.

For the honey mustard spread, combine the mustard, mayonnaise, salt, and pepper in a mixing bowl and stir well.

When ready to serve, spread 1 tablespoon of honey mustard spread onto each slice of bread. Divide the Salmon Tartare evenly among the slices, then cut each slice into bite-size pieces.

Serve immediately.

Yields 32 to 48 bite-size pieces

❋ The Honey Mustard Spread can be made 2 days beforehand, covered, and refrigerated until you're ready.

Feta and Mint Frittata

I don't remember every meal I've ever eaten, but the pleasure of savoring my first frittata is still clear in my mind. It was in Siena, Italy, a long time ago: a soft, comforting egg dish with fresh basil and Romano cheese. You can substitute any cheese or herb you like. It takes only minutes to prepare and is a versatile dish—you can serve it hot for brunch, or when cut into small pieces and offered at room temperature, it becomes a delicious starter with drinks.

2 tablespoons unsalted butter, melted

½ cup dry bread crumbs

2 tablespoons olive oil

2 cups chopped onions

9 large eggs

1 cup heavy cream

¾ cup half-and-half

½ teaspoon kosher salt

¼ teaspoon cayenne pepper

1 cup (7 ounces) crumbled feta cheese

1 cup finely chopped fresh mint leaves

¼ cup grated Parmesan cheese

Preheat the oven to 350°F. Brush a 13 x 9-inch baking pan with the melted butter. Sprinkle the bread crumbs evenly over the bottom of the pan.

Sauté the olive oil and onions in a skillet, over medium heat, for about 10 minutes. Do not let it brown.

In a bowl, whisk together the eggs, cream, half-and-half, salt, and cayenne. Fold in the feta cheese, mint, and sautéed onions. Pour the mixture into the prepared pan. Sprinkle the Parmesan cheese over the top.

Bake 30 to 35 minutes, or until just set. Let cool slightly before cutting.

Yields 6 main-course servings, or 36 bite-size pieces, as a starter

Avocado Mousse and Shrimp on Tortilla Chips

This spicy combination works equally well as an hors d'oeuvre or as a first course.

2 teaspoons fresh lime juice

1 clove garlic, minced

¼ cup fresh cilantro leaves

2 ripe avocados, peeled and pitted

1 teaspoon kosher salt

½ jalapeño pepper, seeded and minced

½ cup chopped onion

½ cup heavy cream

1 bunch cilantro, for garnish

One 7-ounce bag tortilla chips

1½ pounds cooked shrimp (about 30 shrimp)

Combine the lime juice, garlic, cilantro, avocado, salt, jalapeño, and onion in a food processor and process until completely smooth.

Whip the cream until soft peaks hold. Fold the avocado purée into the cream.

To serve as an hors d'oeuvre, line a serving plate with cilantro. Heap each chip with a teaspoon of mousse, then top each with a shrimp and place on the serving plate.

To serve as a first course, line 6 plates with cilantro leaves. Divide the chips, mousse, and shrimp among the plates and serve.

Yields 6 first-course servings, 12 hors d'oeuvres

Soy Bean Hummus with Garlic, Lemon, and Cilantro

This smooth green purée made with soy beans (also called edamame) is great with toasted pita bread or cut-up fresh vegetables: a perfect snack to take to the beach since it tastes best when warmed by the sun.

2 pounds fresh soy beans in pods (2 cups, shelled) or 2 cups frozen beans

1 clove garlic, minced

1½ teaspoons kosher salt

½ teaspoon freshly ground black pepper

¼ cup fresh lemon juice

¼ cup olive oil

2 tablespoons finely chopped fresh cilantro or mint

Place the soy beans in a pot, cover with water, and cook for 12 minutes or until tender. Drain the beans.

Transfer the beans to a food processor. Add the garlic, salt, pepper, and lemon juice and purée for 30 seconds. With the motor running, slowly pour the olive oil through the feed tube in a thin stream. If the mixture seems too thick, add 1 tablespoon water. Add the cilantro and pulse 3 times. Serve at room temperature.

Yields 2½ cups

❦ If covered and refrigerated, the hummus will last up to 3 days.

Hot–Smoked Salmon Toasts with Horseradish Cream and Chives

Hot-smoked salmon is much like cooked salmon except for its subtle smoky taste. You may find it at most seafood markets where it's sold in serving-size pieces with the bones removed and the skin left on.

1 pound hot-smoked salmon
2 tablespoons rice vinegar
½ clove garlic, minced
2 tablespoons olive oil
½ teaspoon kosher salt
½ teaspoon freshly ground black pepper
4 slices sourdough country-style bread
8 ounces cream cheese, softened
⅓ cup heavy cream
1 tablespoon grated fresh horseradish or 2 teaspoons prepared horseradish
3 tablespoons thinly sliced fresh chives

Preheat the oven to 400°F. Remove the skin and dark flesh from the salmon. Cut or flake the fish into 24 pieces. Sprinkle with the vinegar and set it aside.

Mix the garlic, oil, salt, and pepper together and brush over the bread slices. Toast the bread in the hot oven until crisp.

Whip the cream cheese, heavy cream, and horseradish with an electric mixer until the texture is thick. Add 2 tablespoons of the chives and mix only to blend.

Spread the cream cheese mixture evenly over the toasted bread. Cut each slice into 6 pieces. Mound salmon onto each piece and sprinkle with the remaining chives.

Yields 24 bite-size pieces, 6 to 8 servings

Stuffed Eggs

Eggs are the ultimate comfort food and appeal to me in all forms: boiled, fried, scrambled, as omelets, frittatas, or as the chief ingredient in the old reliable quiche. These stuffed eggs, in particular, are a real favorite with my family and my wonderful customers at Loaves and Fishes.

12 eggs

½ cup mayonnaise

1 teaspoon Dijon mustard

½ teaspoon kosher salt

½ teaspoon ground white pepper

½ teaspoon minced garlic

¼ cup minced shallots

2 tablespoons minced curly parsley, plus extra for garnish

⅛ teaspoon hot pepper sauce

Place the eggs in a saucepan, cover with cold water, and bring to a boil. Lower the heat and simmer for 8 minutes.

Drain and cool the eggs under cold running water. Peel the eggs and cut each in half through its equator. Place the yolks in a food processor. Cut a thin slice off the bottom of each egg white so it is able to stand upright and place the whites on a platter.

Add the mayonnaise, mustard, salt, and pepper to the yolks and purée until just smooth.

Combine the garlic, shallots, parsley, and hot pepper sauce in a small bowl. Divide the garlic-shallot mixture equally among the wells of each egg white.

Pipe or spoon the puréed yolk on top of the mixture, mounding each one a little. Garnish with a sprinkling of minced parsley.

Yields 24 stuffed egg halves

❧ Try replacing the garlic-shallot filling with cold foie gras or chicken liver pâté.

❧ Or fold into the yolk mixture:
  • minced anchovies
  • minced ham
  • minced cornichons for a bit of zip
  • ¼ cup salmon roe

Use your taste and imagination to vary this humble stuffed egg.

Smoked and Poached Salmon Hors d'Oeuvres

A delightfully savory spread to go with drinks. Serve with whole-grain bread cut into bite-size pieces, cucumber slices, or thinly sliced French bread, and let everyone help themselves.

1 cup dry white wine

1½ cups water

2 sprigs of fresh thyme

1 bay leaf

6 black peppercorns, crushed

8 ounces fresh salmon fillet

8 ounces smoked salmon, diced

4 tablespoons (2 ounces) unsalted butter, softened

Grated zest of 1 lime

1½ tablespoons fresh lime juice

1½ teaspoons Dijon mustard

½ cup minced shallots

2 teaspoons capers, drained

¼ cup finely chopped fresh dill

¾ teaspoon kosher salt

¾ teaspoon freshly ground black pepper

⅛ teaspoon cayenne pepper

1 teaspoon good brandy

Combine the wine, water, thyme, bay leaf, and peppercorns in a shallow saucepan and bring to a boil. Add the fresh salmon and simmer, covered, for 8 to 10 minutes until the fish is cooked. Drain the salmon and transfer it to a bowl. Set it aside until the fish has reached room temperature.

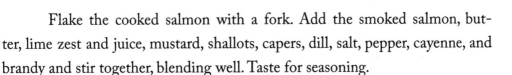

Flake the cooked salmon with a fork. Add the smoked salmon, butter, lime zest and juice, mustard, shallots, capers, dill, salt, pepper, cayenne, and brandy and stir together, blending well. Taste for seasoning.

Chill the spread 5 hours or overnight, remembering that it tastes best served at room temperature.

Yields 4 to 6 servings

✻ This can be made a day ahead, covered, chilled and, for the best results, returned to room temperature before serving.

Spicy Corn Fritters with Salmon Caviar Dip

I have served this easy-to-make elegant dish as a first course, a light lunch, and as part of a festive breakfast. Make sure you buy the freshest, largest salmon eggs from your fish market or specialty food store.

¾ cup coarse cornmeal

¾ cup unbleached all-purpose flour

2 teaspoons baking powder

½ teaspoon kosher salt

¾ teaspoon red pepper flakes

Kernels cut from 2 small ears of corn, about ¾ cup

2 large eggs

1 cup plus 2 tablespoons buttermilk

½ cup chopped fresh chives

¼ cup peanut oil

¼ cup clarified butter

Salmon Caviar Dip

¾ cup sour cream

¾ cup mayonnaise

1 teaspoon hot pepper sauce

⅓ cup chopped fresh chives

¼ cup finely chopped fresh dill

½ teaspoon kosher salt

7 ounces salmon roe

Fresh dill sprigs, for garnish

Combine the cornmeal, flour, baking powder, salt, pepper flakes, and corn in a large bowl. Stir in the eggs, buttermilk, and chives. Set aside for 15 minutes to allow the ingredients to blend.

Combine 1 tablespoon each of the peanut oil and butter in a large heavy skillet over medium-high heat. Tilt the pan to make sure the bottom is coated evenly. When the oil is hot, drop in the corn mixture by tablespoons, 2 inches apart. Fry the fritters 3 to 4 minutes per side, until they turn dark golden brown. Transfer the first batch to a platter and repeat this process until all the batter has been used, adding more peanut oil and butter to the skillet as needed.

To make the salmon caviar dip, combine the sour cream, mayonnaise, hot sauce, chives, dill, salt, and salmon roe in a bowl and stir gently to blend.

Serve the fritters warm with a heaping bowl of salmon caviar dip nearby. Garnish with fresh dill sprigs.

Yields 32 fritters, and 2¼ cups dip, 6 to 8 servings

- The Salmon Caviar Dip is a very popular Loaves and Fishes standard that, as a starter, goes well with fresh-cut vegetables.

- You can adjust the amount of red pepper flakes, less spicy or even more so for those robust types.

Chicken Liver Mousse

This old-fashioned silky smooth pâté can be offered with buttered toast, crunchy French bread, or apple or pear slices. I usually set it on our picnic table and let our guests help themselves while we tend to the grill. Customers often ask how I get the mousse so smooth. The answer is b–u–t–t–e–r!

1 cup chopped onion

2 tablespoons olive oil

1 pound chicken livers, trimmed

3 tablespoons Cognac

2 tablespoons Dijon mustard

2 teaspoons kosher salt

1 teaspoon freshly ground black pepper

¼ teaspoon ground nutmeg

24 tablespoons (12 ounces) unsalted butter, softened

Over medium heat, sauté the onions in the olive oil in a heavy skillet for about 5 minutes until the onions turn glossy. Add the chicken livers and sauté for another 10 minutes, until just cooked. Cool to room temperature.

Transfer the mixture to a food processor, add the Cognac, mustard, salt, pepper, and nutmeg, and process until smooth. Add the butter, 6 tablespoons (3 ounces) at a time, processing each time until the butter is absorbed.

Scrape the mousse into a pretty serving bowl and chill for 2 hours or more before serving.

Yields 6 to 10 servings, depending on appetites

※ You can make this ahead of time. Covered and refrigerated, the mousse can keep for up to 1 week.

Soups

There are many recipes that require a good stock. Nowadays you can buy beef, chicken, and vegetable stocks at just about any supermarket. Some seem too salty for my taste, others too bland. If you don't mind doctoring the stock to your taste, and if you really don't have time to make fresh stock and freeze it for future use, then by all means, make life easier for yourself and buy ready-made stock. However, if there are a couple of rainy spring days strung together with winter's chill still nipping at the windows, making a large pot of your own stock would be just the thing to warm the kitchen and fill it with the most delicious and comforting aromas. Once you've made it, used it, and tasted the difference between fresh and store-bought, I believe you'll be encouraged to make fresh stock more often. Really.

Chicken Stock

We all know that a good chicken stock is the heart of a truly satisfying soup and adds richness to many fine dishes and sauces. To vary the flavor, add a few pieces of fresh ginger to the stock while it cooks and 2 tablespoons of soy sauce at the end of its cooking time.

> 3 pounds chicken backs and necks
>
> 1 very large onion, skin left on, quartered
>
> 1 large carrot, cut into 2-inch pieces
>
> 1 celery stalk, leaves left on, cut into 2-inch pieces
>
> 8 sprigs of flat-leaf parsley
>
> 2 teaspoons kosher salt
>
> 1 teaspoon freshly ground black pepper

Place all the ingredients in a large stockpot. Cover by at least 5 inches with cold water and bring to a boil. Cover the pot loosely and simmer over low heat for 3 hours. Ladle the stock through a fine-mesh strainer. Discard the solids. The stock is now ready to use.

Yields about 3 quarts

※ The stock, in an airtight container, is good refrigerated for up to 3 days and up to 3 months in the freezer. Freeze the stock in 2-cup and 1-quart containers, since those are the amounts usually called for in most recipes. Freeze stock in ice cube trays for even smaller portions to use in sauces and gravies.

Simple Soups and Simple Soup Garnishes

Soup has no season, and is really easy to prepare. Once you have a good stock to work with, the rest is all about personal taste and the creative spirit. Start by sautéing some chopped onions in olive oil, sauté some cut-up vegetables of your choice, add your delicious homemade stock and a splash of Herb-Infused Oil (page 3), let it simmer for about 20 minutes—and there it is. Season it and dress it up with whatever complements the soup: crème fraîche, chopped parsley or dill or mint, minced mushrooms, croutons, or a fresh strawberry. Chilled or heated, this is an almost foolproof design for preparing soup. In the bloom of summer, the colorful soups that pass across your table will excite the eye and tease the palate. Another plus is that soups can be prepared up to three days ahead and kept refrigerated until you're ready to serve them.

Following are three more recipes: one is for the very useful and versatile Crème Fraîche that we use with both savory and sweet recipes and following that, two recipes for the universally adored Crouton, always an asset with soups or salads.

Crème Fraîche

Heat 2 cups heavy cream until very hot but not boiling. Stir in 2 tablespoons buttermilk. Remove from the heat, cover, and let stand at room temperature until its texture becomes very thick. This usually takes 24 hours. Covered and refrigerated it lasts 3 weeks.

Yields 2 cups

Unseasoned Croutons

Cube white bread (with crusts) and lay the pieces on a baking sheet. Toast in a preheated 400°F oven for 10 minutes. Use immediately or cool and store in airtight containers.

Seasoned Croutons

1 teaspoon kosher salt
2 cloves garlic, minced
½ cup olive oil
1 loaf French bread cut into ½-inch cubes, with crusts

Mash the salt and garlic into a paste. Stir in the olive oil. Place the bread cubes in a bowl and drizzle with the oil mixture. Toss to blend well. Place the cubes on a baking sheet and toast in preheated 400°F oven for 10 minutes, or until the croutons turn golden brown. Cool and store in an airtight container.

Chilled Blueberry and Strawberry Soup

A traditional Schleswig-Holstein summer soup, served on festive occasions such as weddings and every year at summer solstice gatherings. Since berries are such a good and delicious source of vitamins, they play an important role in all Scandinavian regions where fresh fruits and vegetables have a very short growing season.

4 cups small, sweet fresh strawberries, washed and hulled

4 cups fresh blueberries, washed and picked over

1 cup sugar

3½ cups water

1 lemon, sliced in 8 wedges

2 short cinnamon sticks

1 cup sour cream or yogurt, *not* low-fat, plus extra for garnish

Extra berries, for garnish

Place the berries, sugar, water, lemon, and cinnamon sticks in a large heavy saucepan and bring to a boil. Lower the heat and simmer, uncovered, for 15 minutes. Chill for 4 hours, or overnight.

When ready, discard the lemon and cinnamon sticks. Using a blender, purée the soup in batches. Pour into a large bowl and, with a wire whisk, blend in the sour cream. Chill several hours, until ready to serve.

Serve cold, garnished with sour cream and fresh berries.

Yields 2½ quarts, 6 to 8 servings

Chilled Tomato-Cucumber Soup with Crouton Garnish

We use large, juicy, very ripe beefsteak tomatoes to make our soup. With crusty bread and an assortment of soft and semi-soft cheeses, this soup makes a very nice unfussy lunch. We also serve it as a delightfully cooling first course.

3 pounds ripe large tomatoes, coarsely chopped

1½ cups chopped onion

2 cups chopped seedless cucumber, skin left on

1 cup chopped red bell pepper

3 cloves garlic, minced

1 cup coarsely chopped white bread (crusts left on)

2 tablespoons red wine vinegar

2 tablespoons fresh lime juice

1 teaspoon sugar

2 teaspoons kosher salt

¾ teaspoon hot pepper sauce

¾ teaspoon ground cumin

½ cup extra virgin olive oil

Garnish

About 4 slices white bread, crusts left on, cubed

1 cup finely chopped seedless cucumber, skin left on

Purée the tomatoes, onions, cucumber, peppers, garlic, bread, vinegar, lime juice, sugar, salt, hot sauce, and cumin in a blender until smooth. You may need to do this in 3 or 4 batches. Transfer the soup to a large bowl and stir in the olive oil. The soup should be covered and chilled for at least 2 hours or overnight.

To make the croutons, preheat the oven to 400°F. Place the cubed bread on a baking sheet and bake for 10 minutes. Allow to cool.

Ladle the soup into individual serving bowls and serve cold with the two garnishes on the side.

Yields 2 quarts, 8 servings as a first course

Creamy Asparagus Soup

This is the ultimate summer soup, combining the freshest herbs, regal asparagus, a hint of garlic, and a pinch of pungent and colorful saffron.

3 tablespoons unsalted butter

1 tablespoon olive oil

2 cups finely chopped onion

1 large clove garlic, minced

1 teaspoon saffron

2 cups peeled and coarsely chopped baking potatoes

5 cups Chicken Stock (page 28)

2 tablespoons finely chopped curly parsley, plus extra for garnish

2 teaspoons finely chopped fresh tarragon

2 teaspoons kosher salt

½ teaspoon ground white pepper

1½ pounds green asparagus, trimmed and cut into 2-inch pieces

¼ cup heavy cream

Melt the butter with the oil in a large heavy soup pot over medium heat. Add the onions, garlic, and saffron and sauté for 4 to 5 minutes, stirring often, until the onions are softened.

Add the potatoes and chicken stock. Bring to a boil. Reduce the heat to medium-low and simmer for 20 minutes.

Stir in the parsley, tarragon, salt, pepper, and asparagus and cook 5 minutes longer. Stir in the cream and set the soup aside for 1 hour to cool.

Pour the soup into a blender and purée until smooth. Depending on the size of your blender, you may have to do this in several batches.

To serve this soup cold, chill it covered for at least 2 hours or overnight. If you reheat it, do not let it boil.

Serve hot or cold, garnished with a sprinkling of chopped parsley.

Yields 6 to 8 servings

Creamed Carrot Soup with Ginger and Lime

Hot or cold, this is a real palate pleaser.

2 cups chopped sweet onion

2 tablespoons olive oil

5 cups peeled and chopped carrots (about 2 pounds)

5 cups Chicken Stock (page 28)

1 cup water

2 tablespoons grated fresh ginger

1 teaspoon kosher salt (omit if using store-bought stock)

½ teaspoon freshly ground black pepper

1 tablespoon plus 1 teaspoon fresh lime juice

1 cup half-and-half

1 tablespoon finely chopped curly parsley

In a large heavy soup pot, sauté the onions in the olive oil over low heat for 5 minutes, until the onions appear glossy. Add the carrots, chicken stock, water, and ginger and bring to a boil. Lower the heat, cover the pot, and let the soup simmer for 30 minutes.

Add the salt if using, pepper, lime juice, half-and-half, and cook, uncovered, for 5 minutes, stirring a few times. Cool to room temperature.

Purée the soup in a blender or food processor. To serve the soup cold, cover and chill it for 2 hours or overnight. If you reheat the soup, do not allow it to boil. Serve hot or cold, garnished with chopped parsley.

Yields 6 mugs or 8 cups

Fresh Corn Soup

Creamy, sweet, with lots of that great fresh corn taste.

1 tablespoon olive oil

2 tablespoons (1 ounce) unsalted butter

3 cups chopped onions

2 tablespoons raw rice

1 large clove garlic, finely chopped

5 cups Chicken Stock (page 28)

4 cups freshly cut corn kernels (about 6 medium ears of corn)

1 teaspoon kosher salt

¾ teaspoon ground white pepper

⅓ cup heavy cream

1 tablespoon fresh lime juice

Crème Fraîche (page 30), for garnish

Chopped fresh chives, for garnish

Heat the oil and butter in a large heavy soup pot over medium heat. Add the onions and sauté for 5 minutes, stirring often, until the onions are soft and glossy. Do not let them brown. Add the rice and garlic and sauté a minute longer. Add the stock and simmer over low heat for 15 minutes.

Add the corn, salt, and pepper. Simmer another 5 minutes. Add the cream and lime juice and stir well. Set it aside to cool.

Using a blender or food processor, purée the soup in batches, then force it through a medium-mesh sieve into a bowl. To serve the soup cold, chill it covered for at least 2 hours or overnight. If you reheat it, do not let it boil. Serve hot or cold. Garnish each serving with a dab of crème fraîche and a pinch of chopped chives.

Yields 6 servings

Pea and Watercress Soup

This soup has a very satisfying taste, especially when you can use freshly picked peas. Their sweetness mixes so well with the peppery taste of watercress. We like topping it off with a dollop of Crème Fraîche (page 30) or sour cream and sprigs of bright green watercress.

2 tablespoons canola oil

2½ cups chopped onions

2 cups peeled and chopped baking potatoes

6 cups Chicken Stock (page 28)

1 cup riesling or other medium-dry white wine

2 teaspoons kosher salt

⅛ teaspoon cayenne pepper

½ teaspoon sugar

2½ cups shelled peas (about 2½ pounds in the pod)

1 bunch fresh bright green watercress, rinsed (6 sprigs saved for garnish)

3 ice cubes

½ cup heavy cream

Heat the oil in a large heavy soup pot. Add the onions and sauté over low heat for about 10 minutes, until soft. Add the potatoes, chicken stock, wine, salt, cayenne, and sugar. Cover and simmer for 25 minutes.

Add the peas and cook, uncovered, for 1 minute only. Add the watercress, stems and all, and cook 1 minute longer. Remove from heat and add the ice cubes to stop the cooking process and to keep the soup a bright green.

Using a food processor, purée the soup in 2 or 3 batches. Return the soup to the pot, add the cream, and stir well. To serve the soup cold, chill it covered for 5 hours or overnight. To serve hot, reheat the soup gently over medium-low heat (do not let it boil).

Serve hot or cold, garnished with watercress sprigs.

Yields 6 servings

❧ If using frozen peas, look for "individually quick frozen" packages of petit pois or English peas.

Cream of Mushroom and Scallion Soup

The combination of wild and cultivated mushrooms creates an intense and richly flavored soup. With crusty bread and a small salad it is a perfect lunch treat, or serve it in small bowls as a first course on a cool summer night.

¼ cup olive oil

4 tablespoons (2 ounces) unsalted butter

4 bunches scallions, trimmed, washed, and chopped (white and green parts)

2½ tablespoons all-purpose flour

8 ounces white button mushrooms, cleaned and chopped

8 ounces cremini mushrooms, cleaned and chopped

4 ounces fresh morels, cleaned

6 cups Chicken Stock (page 28)

¾ cup heavy cream

1 cup flat-leaf parsley, leaves only

Kosher salt and freshly ground black pepper to taste

Heat the oil and butter in a large heavy soup pot over medium heat. Add the scallions and sauté for 5 minutes. Stir in the flour until it is absorbed. Add the mushrooms and chicken stock. Stir once. Cover and cook over low heat for 20 minutes.

Remove from heat. Add the cream and parsley. Purée in batches in a food processor until smooth. Add salt and pepper to taste. Reheat gently; do not let it boil. Serve hot.

Yields 7 cups, 4 servings in bowls or 6 mugs

❧ Garnish with a bit of Crème Fraîche (page 30) and julienne scallion greens or a dollop of sour cream and a sprig of flat-leaf parsley.

❧ If fresh morels are not available, use 2 ounces dried morels. Soak them in 1 cup hot water for 10 minutes before adding them to the soup. Strain the soaking water and add it to the soup.

Corn and Lobster Soup

It is strange to think that at one time lobsters were thought of as poor people's food. This creamy variation of the Puritans' idea of thrifty cooking is now considered something of a luxury. We serve this deliciously gratifying treat on those cool nights in June when the fog rolls in and blankets all of Long Island.

4 tablespoons (2 ounces) unsalted butter

2 cups peeled and finely chopped onions

3 cups peeled and chopped Yukon Gold potatoes in ½-inch pieces

2 cups clam juice

4 cups half-and-half

1 bay leaf

¼ teaspoon cayenne pepper

Kernels cut from 4 ears of fresh corn (about 2 cups)

½ cup heavy cream

12 ounces cooked lobster meat, cut into bite-size pieces

Kosher salt and freshly ground black pepper to taste

1 tablespoon minced fresh parsley, for garnish

Melt the butter in a large heavy soup pot over low heat, and sauté the onions until they are transparent. Add the potatoes, clam juice, half-and-half, bay leaf, and cayenne. Bring to a boil. Lower the heat, cover, and simmer for 15 minutes.

Add the corn and simmer 5 minutes. Add the cream and lobster and simmer until very hot but not boiling. Remove from heat and discard bay leaf. Season with salt and pepper to taste. Garnish with parsley and serve hot.

Yields 6 servings

* You can substitute shrimp or any firm lean white fish, such as angler fish, cod, or halibut for the lobster meat. They all hold up well and are delicious.

Chicken Vegetable Soup

Our selection of take-out foods changes weekly and includes five different soups that vary with the seasons. This chicken soup is always on the list. Our customers are comforted to know that we always have this restorative soup-cure forever at the ready, for whatever ails them.

2 tablespoons (1 ounce) unsalted butter

2 cups chopped onion

1 cup chopped carrots

1½ cups chopped celery

1 cup chopped fennel

2 cups peeled and chopped Yukon Gold potatoes, in ½-inch pieces

2½ quarts Chicken Stock (page 28)

3 cups cooked chicken meat

1 cup shelled peas (1 pound in the pod)

Kosher salt and freshly ground black pepper, to taste

2 tablespoons minced curly parsley

Melt the butter in a large soup pot. Add the onion, carrots, celery, fennel, and potatoes and sauté over medium heat for 5 minutes. Do not let the mixture brown. Add the chicken stock and bring to a boil. Lower heat and let the soup simmer, partly covered, for 20 minutes. Add the chicken and peas. Simmer for 2 more minutes. Season with salt and pepper, sprinkle with parsley, and serve hot.

Yields 6 or more servings

The Bread Basket

We thought it might be helpful to assemble a small variety of easy-to-make breads, muffins, and crisps to augment your picnic basket, fill out your buffet table, and complement soups, salads, and main meals. Included is a simple recipe for the classic popover that not only fits neatly into all the above-mentioned categories but, stuffed with ice cream and drizzled with chocolate, magically transforms into an amazing dessert.

Buttery Cornbread

This is great with soups, salads, and meats, and also with scrambled or fried eggs at breakfast or brunch.

    1¾ cups coarse stone-ground yellow cornmeal

    1½ cups unbleached all-purpose flour

    6 tablespoons sugar

    1 tablespoon baking powder

    1 teaspoon kosher salt

    1¾ cups buttermilk

    12 tablespoons (6 ounces) unsalted butter, melted and cooled

    2 large eggs plus 1 egg yolk, beaten

Combine the cornmeal, flour, sugar, baking powder, and salt in a large bowl. Add the buttermilk, melted butter, and eggs and stir well to blend. Set aside for 30 minutes.

Preheat the oven to 375°F. Butter a 13 x 9 x 2-inch baking pan.

Pour the batter into the pan and bake for 40 to 45 minutes, until the bread is browned around the edges and a tester inserted into the center comes out clean. Cool for 5 minutes. Turn the bread out onto a rack and allow it to cool completely before cutting it into 2-inch squares.

Yields 24 pieces

Popovers

Surprisingly easy and adaptable. Try them stuffed with soft scrambled eggs for breakfast, with butter and preserves, with soups or salads, or, since this is essentially the same recipe as one would use for Yorkshire Pudding, with steaks and roasts. Or try scooping ice cream into each popover, drizzle it with chocolate sauce and serve it as an impressive dessert.

4 tablespoons (2 ounces) butter

4 large eggs

2 cups milk

1¾ cups unbleached all-purpose flour

1 teaspoon kosher salt

Preheat the oven to 450°F.

Melt the butter in a small saucepan. Spoon 1 teaspoon butter into each well of a 12-cup nonstick muffin pan. Discard any unused butter. Place the pan in the oven for 3 minutes to heat.

With a wire whisk, beat the eggs in a medium bowl. Add the milk, flour, and salt. Beat until smooth. Spoon the batter into the heated pan, filling each cup two-thirds full. Bake 15 minutes. Lower the heat to 400°F and bake 15 minutes longer. Do not open the oven door during baking time or the popovers may not rise properly.

Yields 12 popovers

Cheese Crisps

Great with cocktails, starters, appetizers, soups, and salads. Use a freshly grated hard cheese, such as Parmigiano-Reggiano, Romano, or Asiago.

8 ounces freshly grated Parmigiano-Reggiano (about 2 cups)

Preheat the oven to 400°F. Using a tablespoon, distribute mounds of grated cheese onto a parchment-lined baking sheet, spaced 2 to 3 inches apart to give crisps ample room to spread. Pat each mound into a level circle or oblong shape.

Bake 3 to 5 minutes, until crisps become bubbly, lacy, and have turned a light golden hue. Remove from the oven and allow crisps to cool on baking sheet. Remove with a thin spatula and place on racks to cool thoroughly.

Yields about 32 crisps

❧ To store, place the crisps in an airtight container, with wax paper between each layer. These will keep up to a week at room temperature.

❧ For larger crisps use 2 tablespoons per mound and space the crisps, before leveling them, 3 to 4 inches apart. Add a minute onto the baking time.

❧ Flavor the crisps by adding 1 or 2 teaspoons of finely chopped fresh herbs—thyme, rosemary, or chives—or ground black pepper or finely chopped nuts.

Buttermilk Biscuits

Who can resist a hot biscuit, split and spread with butter? These are welcome at breakfast or dinner.

> 2 cups unbleached all-purpose flour
> 2 tablespoons sugar
> 1 tablespoon baking powder
> 8 tablespoons (4 ounces) unsalted butter, softened
> 1 cup buttermilk
> 1 egg yolk
> 2 tablespoons milk

Preheat the oven to 375°F.

Place the flour, sugar, and baking powder in a large bowl and stir. Add the butter and, with your hands, blend the mixture until it is the size of peas. Chill in the freezer for 10 minutes.

Remove and add the buttermilk all at once. Mix quickly until the dough begins to cling together. Turn onto a floured surface. Flatten with the heel of your hand to about ½-inch thickness. Cut into fourteen 2-inch rounds. Place on an ungreased baking sheet. Blend together the egg yolk and milk and brush the tops with the mixture. Bake 18 to 20 minutes.

Yields 14 biscuits

❆ Flavors can be varied by adding fresh herbs such as dill, chives, or rosemary. Or add ½ cup grated sharp Cheddar or grated Parmesan. Stir these into the flour mixture.

Salt-and-Cheese-Crusted Bread Sticks

These are super easy to prepare. Serve them with appetizers, soups, or salads. Take them on picnics, or arrange the sticks in a lovely pitcher to join the array of food on your buffet table.

2 sheets store-bought frozen puff pastry, defrosted but still cold

1 egg white, beaten

1½ teaspoons coarse sea salt

1 cup grated Parmesan cheese, sprinkled on a platter

Preheat the oven to 400°F.

Place the puff pastry on a flat surface. Using a pizza cutter or sharp knife, cut each pastry sheet into seven 2-inch-wide strips. Roll each strip into a thin pipe, then twist each strip, to hold the pastry together. Brush each with egg white. Sprinkle with salt. Roll each in the Parmesan. Place the twists on a parchment-covered baking sheet. Bake 13 to 15 minutes or until golden brown and crisp. They are best served warm, straight from the oven.

Yields 14 bread sticks

❋ These sticks can be prepared, then frozen for up to 2 days. Bake directly from the freezer in a preheated 400°F oven for 18 to 20 minutes.

Tapenade Swirls

This is another great quick appetizer, or a go-with for soups or salads.

1 cup store-bought tapenade
1 cup chopped sun-dried tomatoes (drained if in oil)
1 sheet store-bought frozen puff pastry, defrosted but still cold
Coarse sea salt

In a small bowl blend together the tapenade and tomatoes. Place the puff pastry on a flat work surface. With a pizza cutter or sharp knife, cut the sheet into four equal strips, each about 4 inches wide. Spread the tapenade mixture onto each strip, making sure to leave ½ inch uncovered on the long sides. Starting with a long side, carefully roll the strips into logs. Cover with plastic wrap and freeze.

When ready to bake, preheat the oven to 400°F. Remove the logs from the freezer and unwrap them. Sprinkle them lightly with salt. With a sharp knife, cut the logs into ¼-inch-thick slices. Place the slices flat on a parchment-covered baking sheet, with space between them. Bake for 12 to 15 minutes. Let cool slightly on the pan. Serve warm.

Yields 20 slices

Sandwiches for Beach, Picnic, or Terrace

When Detlef and I first came to this country in 1960, the only bread we were able to find in our tiny New Jersey town was white sandwich bread or soft rye. The breads we were accustomed to had always been made in our own kitchen: sturdy, firm loaves baked with whole grains that we grew on our farm. We made white bread too, semolina rolls, rye breads with or without seeds, all kinds of breads that nowadays you can find in many markets or bakeries.

When we constructed sandwiches at home we used whatever was in our pantry or growing in our garden. There were leftovers, roasted fish and meats; eggs hard-boiled and made into salads; herring, smoked or cured salmon; and many cheeses that we made and ripened in our kitchen. Our garden yielded beans, corn, cucumbers, radishes, tomatoes, lettuces, peas, carrots, beets, rutabagas, onions, dill, parsley, and chives. As you can see, we had many possibilities when it came to creating a sandwich.

But hands down, Americans make the best sandwiches. What a variety! What generous proportions! Our grandson Kyle, born and bred here, after having returned home from a visit to family and friends in Holland, said, "Oma? I ordered a sandwich in Amsterdam and all I got was a little one with almost nothing on it."

And now, with the arrival of the panini sandwich press, it is easy to see how the creative spirit could go wild. There is no secret to a panini sandwich—it's your taste and cravings that determine how big, how small, what shape and size it can be, and whether or not your panini press is large enough to heat the sandwich through. Everyone, I think, loves the grill marks the press imbeds on the outside of the bread. I have a friend who has only a grill pan, stovetop, and a brick and has been making paninis for years. When the brick isn't pressing sandwiches, it serves as a doorstop.

My family loves sandwiches at home, so in the following section, I'd like to share those that we like best. Some are closed, some are on kaiser rolls or French bread, some are open-face Danish sandwiches, called *smørrebrød*, that may require a knife and fork. I am including variations on the traditional grilled burger and others that are favorites from our Loaves and Fishes take-out department.

One night I caught my husband, Detlef, raiding the refrigerator. He had a ton of food spread across the counter and bread teetering in a pile right in front of him. "What in the world are you doing?" I asked. He gave me a smile and replied, "I think I may be constructing an architectural masterpiece!"

Grilled Eggplant, Pepper, and Soppressata Sandwiches

A popular lunch item because it travels well without refrigeration. It can last up to 3 hours at room temperature, or in a cooler, up to 8 hours.

    1 medium eggplant
    2 red bell peppers
    Olive oil
    Kosher salt and freshly ground black pepper to taste
    1 baguette cut into 4 equal pieces and split
    ½ cup mayonnaise
    16 thin slices soppressata
    ¼ cup chopped fresh basil leaves

Slice the eggplant into 8 rounds. Cut the peppers lengthwise into quarters. Brush the vegetables with olive oil and season with salt and pepper. Place on a hot grill and cook 10 minutes, turning with tongs from side to side, until vegetables are nicely browned.

Spread mayonnaise on the baguette halves. Place 2 slices each of eggplant and pepper per sandwich. Top each with 4 slices of soppressata. Sprinkle with chopped basil.

Serve warm, perfect for picnicking.

Yields 4 sandwiches

Egg Salad, Radish, and Sprout Sandwiches

Radishes and sprouts add a special crispness to this old standard. The egg salad can be made early in the day, and the sandwiches assembled at serving time. Cut these into mini sandwiches and they turn into delicious hors d'oeuvres. You can double the ingredients to make 8 sandwiches.

6 eggs
¼ cup minced onion
½ cup finely chopped celery
¾ cup mayonnaise
½ teaspoon kosher salt
½ teaspoon freshly ground black pepper
1 teaspoon Dijon mustard
8 slices white sandwich bread
8 large red radishes, sliced
1 container fresh radish or alfalfa sprouts

Place the eggs in a medium saucepan, cover with cold water, and bring to a boil. Lower the heat and simmer for 8 minutes. Drain and cool. Peel, then chop the eggs in a bowl.

Add the onion, celery, ⅓ cup of the mayonnaise, salt, pepper, and mustard. Stir to blend well.

Spread the remaining mayonnaise over the bread slices. Scoop egg salad onto 4 slices, arrange radish slices over the egg salad, and top with sprouts. Top with the remaining bread slices. Cut in half and serve.

Yields 4 full-size servings or 16 hors d'oeuvres

Smoked Turkey and Cheddar Cheese Panini

A great blending of tastes: sharp Cheddar, smoked turkey, the bite of creamy horseradish, and the fresh taste of arugula make this an extraordinary sandwich.

1 cup loosely packed arugula leaves, well-washed and dried

1 cup mayonnaise

1 tablespoon prepared horseradish

½ teaspoon kosher salt

½ teaspoon freshly ground black pepper

12 slices rustic-style bread

1½ pounds smoked turkey (12 thick slices)

¾ pound sharp Cheddar cheese (6 thick slices)

Preheat a panini press.

Using a food processor, finely chop the arugula. Add the mayonnaise, horseradish, salt, and pepper and mix. Spread the mixture on one side of all 12 bread slices. Cover 6 bread slices with turkey, top with Cheddar cheese, and cover with remaining bread slice, mayonnaise side down. Cut each sandwich in half and grill in the panini press for 3 to 5 minutes, or until bread is light brown, the interior is warm, and the cheese is melted.

Yields 6 sandwiches

❋ Have your deli slice the cheddar and smoked turkey for you.

Barbecue Sauced Chicken Sandwiches

This has to be the ultimate make-ahead, one-dish meal; the recipe can be doubled to feed a crowd. When our children were teenagers, we often had four to six hungry ones around the house at lunchtime. Now it's an even bigger hit with our teenage grandchildren. The only things that have changed are the title, and the meat. Thirty years ago they were called Sloppy Joes and were made with ground beef.

2 cups finely chopped onion

3 cloves garlic, minced

¼ cup olive oil

1½ cups ketchup

1 cup chili sauce

1 cup water

3 tablespoons red wine vinegar

1 tablespoon Worcestershire sauce

2 tablespoons light brown sugar

1½ teaspoons kosher salt

2 pounds skinned and boned chicken breast, cut into 2 x 1-inch strips

4 large garden lettuce leaves

4 large kaiser rolls or English muffins, split and toasted

¼ cup finely chopped fresh chives

Sauté the onion and garlic in the olive oil for 5 minutes in a large heavy saucepan over medium heat. Stir often so it does not brown. Stir in the ketchup, chili sauce, water, vinegar, Worcestershire, sugar, and salt, and let it simmer for 5 minutes. Add the chicken strips, stir to combine, cover and simmer for another 12 minutes. Taste and adjust the seasoning.

To serve, place a lettuce leaf on the bottom of each roll, spoon chicken over the lettuce, and garnish with chives. Top with the other half of the roll.

Yields 4 sandwiches

❉ Adding 2 extra rolls can stretch the servings from 4 to 6.

Warm Tuna Sandwich with Ginger-Lemon Sauce

I was first introduced to tuna salad sandwiches many years ago when a new friend invited me and my two small children to lunch. She spoke a little German and I a little English. She turned white tuna from a can into a memorable sandwich that remains a family stand-by. Then one day, on our travels, I got brave and ordered raw tuna. I fell in love with its flavor and texture and the soy-ginger sauce that went along with it. This burger is a Fourth of July "cook-out special" at our house.

2 pounds fresh sushi grade tuna

1½ teaspoons grated fresh ginger

1 teaspoon chili paste (see note)

2 tablespoons fish sauce (see note)

2 teaspoons kosher salt

1 teaspoon freshly ground black pepper

2 teaspoons toasted sesame oil (see note)

2 large eggs

½ cup dry bread crumbs

4 to 6 Kaiser rolls, split and grilled or toasted

Lettuce leaves, for serving

Sliced ripe tomatoes, for serving

Thinly sliced red onions, for serving

Ginger-Lemon Sauce

2 egg yolks

2 tablespoons fresh lemon juice

2 tablespoons grated fresh ginger

1 clove garlic, minced

1 tablespoon Dijon mustard

½ teaspoon hot pepper sauce

1½ teaspoons toasted sesame oil

¾ cup safflower oil

¾ cup olive oil

¼ cup heavy cream

½ teaspoon kosher salt

Cut the tuna into large chunks and pulse 3 or 4 times in the food processor. Do not chop any longer or the tuna will turn into a paste. Place tuna in a large mixing bowl and add the ginger, chili paste, fish sauce, salt, pepper, sesame oil, eggs, and bread crumbs. Mix with your hands, just to blend. Shape tuna into 6 patties, each about 1½ inches thick. Place patties on a plate, cover and refrigerate for 30 minutes or more.

Preheat the grill to high.

To make ginger-lemon sauce, place the egg yolks, lemon juice, ginger, garlic, mustard, hot pepper sauce, and sesame oil in a food processor. With the motor running, add the safflower and olive oils by droplets. When the sauce starts to thicken, add the remaining oil in a thin, steady stream. Add the cream and salt. The sauce will have the consistency of mayonnaise. Transfer the sauce to a bowl.

Place the patties on the hot grill, and cook 2 to 3 minutes per side until golden brown outside and rare on the inside. Serve on the rolls with the ginger-lemon sauce, a platter of lettuce leaves, sliced fresh tomatoes, and thinly sliced sweet red onions.

Yields 4 to 6 sandwiches

⁂ Fresh chili paste, fish sauce, and toasted sesame oil are available in the Asian food departments of most supermarkets.

Warm Tilapia with Tartar Sauce on French Bread

Tilapia, farm-raised or imported, is a mild-tasting lean fish that is a wonderful choice for a sandwich, especially when it's served warm. Try it for brunch, lunch, or dinner.

Tartar Sauce

1 cup mayonnaise

¼ cup minced flat-leaf parsley

2 tablespoons minced shallots

3 tablespoons capers, drained and finely chopped

3 tablespoons finely chopped cornichons

Juice of ½ a lemon

Kosher salt and freshly ground black pepper to taste

½ cup mayonnaise

1 teaspoon Dijon mustard

1 teaspoon fresh lemon juice

1½ pounds tilapia fillets (4 fillets, same size)

1½ cups panko or dry bread crumbs

⅓ cup sesame seeds

1½ teaspoons kosher salt

1½ teaspoons freshly ground black pepper

2 tablespoons (1 ounce) unsalted butter

2 tablespoons peanut oil

4 French bread rolls, split

To make the tartar sauce, combine all the ingredients in a small bowl and stir well. Taste for seasoning. Refrigerate until needed.

For the fish, stir the mayonnaise, mustard, and lemon juice together and rub the mixture into both sides of each fillet. Combine the panko, sesame seeds, salt, and pepper and sprinkle the mixture onto a flat plate.

Heat the butter and peanut oil in a large skillet.

Dip the fish fillets into the crumb mixture, coating both sides and carefully place each into the heated oil. Sauté over medium high heat for a total of 10 to 12 minutes, turning once.

Spread tartar sauce on the rolls, stuff each roll with hot, freshly cooked tilapia, and serve.

Yields 4 servings

❈ The Tartar Sauce can be made up to 2 days before needed and can be used as a spread or a sauce. And if you wish, plain mayonnaise can be substituted for the Tartar Sauce.

Open-Faced Shrimp Sandwiches Topped with Salmon Caviar

Belegtes brot, covered bread, is consumed daily by thousands of Germans and Danes who live in the border region where I come from. It is also called smørrebrød, *buttered bread, in Danish and consists of one slice of bread, always buttered, topped with whatever is in the pantry or refrigerator, and eaten with a knife and fork.*

4 slices whole-grain bread

4 tablespoons (2 ounces) softened unsalted butter or 4 tablespoons mayonnaise

1 pound tiny cooked shrimp

1 tablespoon fresh lemon juice

2 tablespoons finely chopped fresh dill

4 lettuce leaves

¼ cup large salmon roe

4 sprigs of dill, for garnish

1 lemon, quartered, for garnish

Spread the bread slices with the butter or mayonnaise. Combine the shrimp, lemon juice, and dill in a bowl. Top each bread slice with a lettuce leaf and one-quarter of the shrimp, then top with a tablespoon of salmon roe. Garnish with dill sprigs and lemon wedges.

Yields 4 sandwiches

Using your imagination and taste, you can create many more combinations to serve as lunch, a cold supper or, when cut into bite-size pieces, as appetizers. For four slices of bread:

- 8 pieces pickled herring, 8 onion rings, and 4 wedges of tomato, on whole-grain bread
- 2 fillets of smoked herring, topped with 8 tablespoons chopped red onion and scrambled eggs, on rye bread
- 12 slices salami or 8 slices of ham, topped with 8 raw onion rings and 8 tablespoons blue cheese, on sourdough bread
- 8 slices smoked salmon, thinly sliced and arranged in overlapping layers, topped with 4 tablespoons sour cream and 1 tablespoon chives, on white bread

Beef Burgers with Grilled Red Onion and Gorgonzola Sauce

A juicy grilled hamburger on a toasted bun, grilled onions, maybe some lettuce and sliced ripe tomatoes, and a creamy gorgonzola sauce to give it that extra special touch. We usually serve these with a platter of corn on the cob, piled high and drizzled with fresh butter.

Gorgonzola Sauce

½ cup minced shallots

¾ cup dry white wine

1½ cups heavy cream

4 ounces Gorgonzola cheese, cut into small pieces

½ teaspoon freshly ground black pepper

Burgers

2 pounds ground beef chuck or sirloin

2 tablespoons coarsely ground black pepper

2 tablespoons olive oil

2 red onions, peeled, cut into ¼-inch slices

6 hamburger buns

For the Gorgonzola sauce, combine the shallots and wine in a small heavy saucepan and cook over medium-high heat for 7 to 8 minutes, until mixture is reduced to ¼ cup. Add the cream and cook until liquid is reduced to 1 cup or until it thickens slightly. Add the Gorgonzola and pepper and cook over low heat for 2 minutes, stirring, until the cheese is melted. Set it aside.

For the burgers, heat the grill to medium-high. Without overworking the meat, shape the beef into 6 patties. Sprinkle the patties on both sides with the coarse pepper and brush both sides with olive oil. Place on the grill for 4 minutes. Turn the patties and grill 4 to 5 minutes longer for medium rare. Meanwhile, brush the onion slices with oil and grill until brown and tender. Grill the buns to crisp lightly.

Serve the patties on a platter with the toasted buns, grilled onions, and reheated Gorgonzola sauce on the side.

Yields 6 beef burgers

⁂ Do not compress the meat while shaping burgers since it breaks down the fat and will dry out the meat: this I learned from James Beard while attending his cooking school.

⁂ The sauce can be made 2 hours ahead of time and reheated.

Grilled Lamb Patties with Mint Tzatziki and Feta in Pita Pockets

It would be best to prepare the tzatziki sauce first, since it should be chilled until ready to use. We make these lamb patties throughout the summer and, believe me, they are always an enormous hit with all ages.

Mint Tzatziki

1 small, seedless cucumber halved lengthwise, center scooped out

1 clove garlic, minced

2 teaspoons distilled white vinegar

1 cup Greek-style yogurt

½ cup sour cream

1½ teaspoons kosher salt

¾ teaspoon hot pepper sauce

2 tablespoons minced fresh mint leaves

Lamb Patties

2 pounds lean, ground lamb, from the hind leg

½ cup minced shallots

2 cloves garlic, minced

¼ cup minced fresh mint leaves

2 teaspoons kosher salt

1½ teaspoons freshly ground black pepper

2 tablespoons cold water

2 tablespoons olive oil

6 pita breads with pockets, top third removed

1 cup crumbled feta cheese (about 6 ounces)

1½ cups shredded lettuce leaves

Using the large holes of a grater, shred the cucumber. You should have about 2 cups. Press liquid out of the shredded cucumber and place in a bowl. Add the garlic, vinegar, yogurt, sour cream, salt, hot sauce, and mint and stir to blend. Chill until needed.

Preheat the grill to medium-high.

Place the lamb in a mixing bowl. Add the shallots, garlic, mint, salt, pepper, and water. Mix with your hands, just to combine. Shape into 6 round patties. Brush each with olive oil and place on the grill for 12 minutes, turning once, for medium-rare.

Meanwhile, grill the pita bread over indirect heat, for only a few minutes, just to warm.

To serve, spoon tzatziki sauce into each pita pocket, tuck a lamb patty inside, add feta and shredded lettuce and serve with the remaining sauce on the side.

Yields 6 servings

Roast Beef Sandwiches with Cilantro Mayonnaise

This, hands down, has been voted the favorite lunch sandwich by my four grandchildren, all teenagers with very healthy appetites. They always ask for pickles and potato salad to complete this meal.

1 clove garlic, minced

¼ cup packed cilantro leaves, minced

1 cup mayonnaise

Four 6-inch sections French bread, split

1 pound thinly sliced roast beef (store-bought)

3 large tomatoes, thinly sliced

Kosher salt and freshly ground black pepper to taste

4 large lettuce leaves

Stir together the garlic, cilantro, and mayonnaise. Spread this onto the 8 bread sections. Arrange the roast beef and tomato slices on the bottom half of the bread. Sprinkle with salt and pepper, top with lettuce, cover with the other bread half and serve.

Yields 4 sandwiches

Salads, Sides, and Go-Withs

*S*alads can be served in a multiple of ways; as sides, light lunches, or as go-withs for soups. By adding meat, fish, or cheese, you can turn them into heartier meals that can serve as gratifying main courses.

The summer months offer us such a brilliant assortment of fresh produce. The lusciously sweet tomato immediately comes to mind: richly red or yellow or orange, some large, some small, some shaped like other fruits (cherries, grapes, and now, strawberry-shaped tomatoes), and always absolutely rewarding. In the height of summer, the vision of tomatoes erected into pyramids at stands all along our country roads is truly remarkable. Tomatoes seem best when they are locally grown and vine ripened. You can tell a good tomato by how firm it is to the touch. It shouldn't be hard and should have a good tomato aroma. It will keep for two or three days, sometimes longer, and should be stored in a shady spot in your kitchen, never in the refrigerator, which robs the tomato of its succulent, distinctive taste.

Fresh greens, herbs, and vegetables are plentiful this time of year and can be mixed and matched by color, texture, and preference. The choices are immense and experimenting is such fun!

The following salad recipes come directly from our kitchen at Loaves and Fishes.

Loaves and Fishes Vinaigrettes

We make these three vinaigrettes by the gallon; they dress salads consisting of green and red leaf lettuce, arugula, romaine, Boston, and baby spinach; we usually use three types of greens in a salad. Sliced red onions, figs, peaches, dried cranberries, or fresh pears cut into small chunks are all tasty additions as are toasted pecans, hazelnuts, or pine nuts. Always go for the freshest ingredients and you cannot miss.

Balsamic Vinaigrette

3 tablespoons good-quality balsamic vinegar

1 clove garlic, minced

½ teaspoon kosher salt

½ teaspoon freshly ground black pepper

½ cup olive oil

Red Wine Vinaigrette

¼ cup red wine vinegar

1 clove garlic, minced

½ teaspoon kosher salt

½ teaspoon hot pepper sauce

½ teaspoon sugar

¾ cup olive oil

White Wine Vinaigrette

¼ cup white wine vinegar

1 small shallot, minced

1 teaspoon Dijon mustard

½ teaspoon kosher salt

¾ teaspoon ground white pepper

½ teaspoon sugar

¾ cup olive oil

Combine the ingredients in a food processor until smooth. All can be made a day ahead and stored at room temperature.

Yields ¾ cup to 1 cup dressing

⚜ I recommend either using these dressings right away or storing them at room temperature for a day, maybe two at the most. I don't recommend refrigerating these dressings. In fact, I strongly urge you not to; when chilled, the oil congeals and the flavors suffer.

Walnut Oil Dressing

This is especially good on strong-tasting herbs and greens such as watercress, endive, radicchio, fresh basil leaves, flat-leaf parsley, mizuna, and escarole.

¼ cup sherry vinegar

1 small shallot, minced

½ teaspoon kosher salt

½ teaspoon freshly ground black pepper

¼ cup walnut oil

¼ cup olive oil

Blend all the ingredients in a food processor until smooth.

Yields about 1 cup

⚘ The dressing can be made a few hours before you dress the greens of your choice. Any leftover dressing stored at room temperature should be used within 2 days.

Bacon-Balsamic Vegetable Dressing

This complements an array of summer and late summer vegetables such as broccoli, aspara-gus, green beans, cauliflower, and Brussels sprouts, each cooked al dente.

8 slices bacon

3 small shallots, chopped fine

6 tablespoons balsamic vinegar

¼ cup fresh lemon juice

1 teaspoon Dijon mustard

¾ cup olive oil

½ teaspoon kosher salt

1 teaspoon freshly ground black pepper

Sauté the bacon in a skillet until crisp. Drain on paper towels, then crumble. Discard all but 2 tablespoons of the bacon fat and sauté the shallots in the same skillet until crisp. Set aside.

Process the balsamic vinegar, lemon juice, mustard, oil, salt, and pepper in a food processor until smooth. Use what you need to lightly coat your vegetables. Sprinkle with the reserved bacon and shallots and serve.

Yields about 1½ cups

⁂ This makes a lot of dressing. Any leftovers stored at room temperature should be used within 2 days.

Roquefort Cheese Dressing

We enjoy this on sun-warmed thinly sliced garden-fresh tomatoes and roasted sweet onions.

>   1 cup crumbled Roquefort cheese (about 6 ounces)
>
>   ½ cup mayonnaise
>
>   1 cup sour cream
>
>   1 tablespoon olive oil
>
>   2 tablespoons Champagne vinegar
>
>   ¼ cup milk
>
>   1 tablespoon vin santo or brandy
>
>   ½ teaspoon cayenne pepper, or to taste

Place ½ cup of the Roquefort in a food processor. Add the mayonnaise, sour cream, olive oil, vinegar, milk, vin santo, and cayenne and pulse 5 to 6 times just to blend. Scrape the mixture into a small bowl. Fold in the remaining ½ cup Roquefort and serve. Cover and store any leftovers in the refrigerator. This dressing can last up to one week.

Yields 2¾ cups

$\mathcal{G}$rilled Lobster with Chili Butter

Open-Faced Shrimp Sandwich topped with Salmon Caviar served
alongside Chilled Blueberry and Strawberry Soup

Parmesan-Panko Crusted Chicken with Black Bean–Avocado Salsa

Warm Tuna Sandwich with Ginger-Lemon Sauce and Pea and Watercress Soup

Frozen Raspberry Mousse, Frozen Orange Mousse, and Baked
Chocolate Pudding with Chantilly Cream

*S*tuffed Eggs; Soybean Hummus with Garlic, Lemon, and Cilantro on Pita Chips; Feta and Mint Frittata; Hot Smoked Salmon Toasts with Horseradish Cream and Chives; Spicy Corn Fritters with Salmon Caviar Dip (*clockwise from left*)

$\mathcal{G}$rilled Tenderloin of Beef with Fresh Herb Sauce complemented by
Asparagus Salad with Roasted Peppers and Goat Cheese

Peach Tart with Almond Topping and a Cookie Crust

Sweet Corn and Tomato Salad with Fresh Cilantro

Made with corn and tomatoes fresh from local farms, this salad is a definite must!

6 ears of fresh corn, husked

1½ pounds plum tomatoes, cut into ½-inch cubes

¾ cup finely chopped red onion

½ cup chopped fresh cilantro

¼ cup extra virgin olive oil

1 tablespoon red wine vinegar

Kosher salt and freshly ground black pepper to taste

Cook the corn in a large pot of boiling salted water for 5 minutes, until just tender. Drain. Cool to room temperature.

Cut the kernels from the cobs and place them in a large bowl. Add the tomatoes, onion, cilantro, olive oil, and vinegar, and toss to blend. Season with salt and pepper.

Yields 6 servings

※ This can be made 2 hours ahead. Let it stand at room temperature, tossing occasionally.

Seedless Cucumber Salad, Scandinavian-Style

A sweet and sour, oh-so-easy-salad that seems to go with everything.

2 seedless cucumbers, unpeeled, very thinly sliced

1 tablespoon kosher salt

½ cup distilled white vinegar

¼ cup finely chopped fresh dill

¼ cup sugar

½ teaspoon freshly ground black pepper

Place the sliced cucumbers in a colander, sprinkle with salt, toss to coat, and set aside for 15 minutes. Give them an occasional stir to distribute the salt.

Combine the vinegar, dill, sugar, and pepper in a large bowl. Stir until the sugar has completely dissolved.

Drain the cucumbers and pat well to dry. Add to the dressing and stir to blend well. Refrigerate at least 15 minutes or up to 2 hours. Serve cold.

Yields 6 to 8 servings

Carrot, Mango, and Apple Slaw

Tangy and crunchy, this splendid little salad is great with Shrimp Cakes (page 174) or any other fish dish. On the farm where I grew up, this was a standard once-a-week salad, minus the mango. I had never seen or tasted a mango until I moved to the States. Now it's become one of my favorite fruits. This salad is as good the day after as the day it's made.

> 4 medium carrots
>
> 1 mango, a bit underripe
>
> 1 apple, such as Golden Delicious
>
> ¼ cup fresh lime juice
>
> 1 teaspoon sugar
>
> 1 teaspoon kosher salt
>
> ½ teaspoon freshly ground black pepper

Trim and peel the carrots. Peel the mango and cut the flesh from the pit. Peel and core the apple and cut into quarters. Grate the carrots, mango, and apple with your food processor. Transfer all to a bowl and sprinkle with the lime juice, sugar, salt, and pepper. Toss gently and serve.

Yields 4 to 6 servings

Red Beet, Teardrop Tomato, and Radicchio Salad

This all-red salad combines the sweetness of beets and tomatoes, the subtle bitterness of radicchio, the crunch of sweet onions, and the aromatic flavoring of aged balsamic. It's a winning combination of taste, texture, and color.

1 pound red beets (4 medium)

2 cups red teardrop or grape tomatoes

1 small head radicchio, cut into 1-inch chunks

⅓ cup thinly sliced red onion

¼ cup aged balsamic vinegar

¼ cup olive oil

¾ teaspoon kosher salt

1 teaspoon freshly ground black pepper

Trim the beets and place them in a medium saucepan. Cover with cold water and bring to a boil. Lower the heat and simmer 30 minutes, until the beets are tender. Drain and cool until easy to handle. Peel the beets and cut into bite-size pieces.

Place the beets, tomatoes, radicchio, and onion in a salad bowl. Drizzle with the vinegar and oil and sprinkle with salt and pepper. Toss to coat all.

Yields 6 or more servings

❧ The salad tastes best if it is given 30 minutes to marinate. It also can be made up to 2 days ahead of time, covered, and stored in the refrigerator. Bring it to room temperature before serving.

Fresh Green Peas and Sugar Snap Peas in Sesame Dressing

When peas show up in early summer, indulge—as in this easy-to-prepare, goes-with-everything salad.

> 3 cups fresh shelled peas (about 3 pounds in pods)
> 12 ounces sugar snap peas, trimmed, strings removed

Sesame Dressing

> 2 tablespoons unseasoned rice vinegar
>
> 1 tablespoon soy sauce
>
> 2 teaspoons toasted sesame oil
>
> 1 packed tablespoon light brown sugar
>
> 1 teaspoon kosher salt
>
> ½ teaspoon freshly ground black pepper

Cook the shelled peas in a large saucepan of boiling salted water for 1 minute, until the peas are almost tender. Add the sugar snap peas and boil for 30 seconds longer. Drain. Rinse the peas under cold running water, to stop the cooking process. Drain again and transfer the peas to a large bowl.

For the Sesame Dressing, blend the vinegar, soy sauce, sesame oil, sugar, salt, and pepper in a small bowl and drizzle it over the peas. Toss to coat. Season with more salt and pepper to taste. Serve at room temperature.

Yields 6 servings

Potato-Corn Salad

We've combined two of summer's favorite picnic foods with wonderful results. Over the years this salad has accompanied many people on picnics and beach parties where arguments still continue on whose potato salad is the best. Here's the most popular one we sell at Loaves and Fishes.

2 pounds medium Yukon Gold or any firm yellow potatoes

½ cup warm Chicken Stock (page 28)

4 ears of fresh corn, husked

⅔ cup chopped fresh chives

⅓ cup chopped fresh dill

1 tablespoon kosher salt

½ cup olive oil

¼ cup white wine vinegar

¼ cup heavy cream

2 teaspoons sugar

¼ teaspoon cayenne pepper

½ teaspoon freshly ground black pepper

Halve the potatoes, place in a medium saucepan, cover with cold water, and bring to a boil. Simmer over medium heat for 10 to 15 minutes until the potatoes are tender. Drain.

When the potatoes are cool enough to handle, peel and slice them into a large bowl. Sprinkle with the warm chicken stock.

Cook the corn in boiling water for 5 minutes. Cool under cold running water. Slice the kernels from the ears and add to the potatoes. Add the chives, dill, and salt.

Combine the olive oil, vinegar, cream, sugar, cayenne, and black pepper in a jar with a tight-fitting lid and shake well to blend. Pour the dressing over the salad and toss gently. Serve at room temperature.

Yields 6 servings

Potato Salad with Radishes and Fresh Dill

A wonderful salad, made even more savory by adding capers and their brine.

2 pounds Yukon Gold or any firm yellow potatoes

¾ cup sliced small red radishes

1 cup finely chopped scallions (white and green parts)

2 tablespoons chopped capers

3 hard-boiled eggs, peeled and chopped

¾ cup mayonnaise

1 teaspoon Dijon mustard

3 tablespoons fresh lemon juice

1 tablespoon caper brine

2 teaspoons kosher salt

½ teaspoon cayenne pepper

¼ cup packed chopped fresh dill

Halve the potatoes. Place in a saucepan, cover with cold water, and bring to a boil. Lower the heat and simmer 15 to 20 minutes, or until tender. Drain. When the potatoes are cool enough to handle, peel, and slice them into a large bowl. Add the radishes, scallions, capers, and eggs.

In another bowl, combine the mayonnaise with the mustard, lemon juice, caper brine, salt, and cayenne. Spoon mixture over the potatoes and toss gently to blend. Cover and chill. For best results, bring to room temperature and add the fresh dill just before serving.

Yields 4 to 6 servings

Thai Noodles

We sell gallons of this fabulous salad all summer long at Loaves and Fishes. I have no idea what makes this noodle dish Thai. A customer gave it this name and it stuck.

> 1 pound capellini
> ¼ cup peanut oil
> ¼ cup soy sauce
> ⅓ cup rice vinegar
> 2 teaspoons toasted sesame oil
> 1 tablespoon sugar
> 1 teaspoon red pepper flakes
> 2 teaspoons minced fresh ginger
> 1 teaspoon minced garlic
> 1 tablespoon kosher salt
> 1½ cups coarsely chopped radicchio
> ½ cup chopped scallions (white and green parts)
> ⅓ cup finely chopped cilantro

Cook the capellini according to package directions, 7 or 8 minutes. Drain and place in a large bowl.

Place the peanut oil, soy sauce, vinegar, sesame oil, sugar, pepper flakes, ginger, garlic, and salt in a food processor fitted with a steel blade and process for 30 seconds.

Pour the dressing over the noodles and mix thoroughly to coat all the pasta strands. Add the radicchio, scallions, and cilantro. Mix just to blend. Serve at room temperature.

Yields 6 to 8 servings

If you dislike cilantro or if it is unavailable at your greengrocer or market, try other herbs in its place such as flat-leaf parsley or dill. Dill works really well with this noodle dish and turns it into a perfect side with about any fish course.

Orange Rice Salad

A truly refreshing, all-seasons side. During the summer, serve the salad at room temperature; in cold weather, omit the dressing, add a handful of raisins, and serve the rice hot.

2 tablespoons olive oil

2 tablespoons unsalted butter

2 cups finely chopped onion

1½ cups long-grain white rice

1½ cups fresh orange juice

1½ cups water

2 teaspoons kosher salt

2 teaspoons ground white pepper

¼ cup toasted pine nuts

1 cup finely chopped celery

¼ cup minced fresh chives or scallion greens

Dressing

¼ cup fresh orange juice

3 tablespoons fresh lemon juice

¼ cup olive oil

½ teaspoon sugar

½ teaspoon kosher salt

½ teaspoon ground white pepper

In a heavy pot over low heat melt the butter with the olive oil and sauté the onions and rice for 5 minutes. Stir often, so it does not brown. Add the orange juice, water, salt, and pepper. Cover and cook 15 to 17 minutes or until rice is just tender. Spoon the rice into a large bowl. Fluff it with a fork to separate the grains. Add the pine nuts, celery, and chives.

Place all the dressing ingredients in a jar with a tight-fitting lid and shake well to blend. Pour dressing over the rice and toss gently but thoroughly. Let cool to room temperature before serving.

Yields 4 to 6 servings

※ If you don't mind the little black specks, by all means use black pepper; it has more flavor. I use white pepper because my then-four-year-old granddaughter, Karina, looking at the rice I put on her plate, said, "Oma, there are tiny bugs in my rice!"

Wheat Berries with Cucumber and Mint

This side dish has a delightfully chewy texture and, with all the colorful fruits and herbs, creates a pretty presentation. Since the wheat berries need to be soaked for 6 hours or overnight, it would be wise to prepare this the day before, cover, and refrigerate it, remembering that it should be brought to room temperature before serving. It's best that way.

1 cup wheat berries

2 cups chopped seedless unpeeled cucumber

2 cups chopped fresh ripe pineapple

1 cup dried cranberries or dried cherries

6 scallions, chopped fine (white and green parts)

1 cup loosely packed, finely chopped fresh mint leaves

¼ cup finely chopped curly parsley

1 clove garlic, mashed

1 tablespoon kosher salt

1 teaspoon freshly ground black pepper

2 tablespoons fresh lemon juice

¼ cup olive oil

Place the wheat berries in a very large stock pot. Add 1½ quarts cold water and bring to a boil. Turn off the heat, cover the pot, and soak the berries overnight in the refrigerator.

When ready, cook the wheat berries for 25 minutes. Drain and transfer to a large bowl. Add the cucumber, pineapple, cranberries, scallions, mint, parsley, garlic, salt, pepper, lemon juice, and olive oil and toss to blend well.

Yields 6 servings

The reason we point out the need for a very large pot is because wheat berries tend to swell many times their original volume. At Loaves and Fishes, a quart of wheat berries seems so insignificant way down at the bottom of our largest 6-quart stock pot, but by morning, when we arrive and remove the lid, the wheat berries have swelled right up to the top rim.

Couscous, Almonds, Raisins, and Mint

We often serve this tasty side with our Butterflied Leg of Lamb (page 140), but it goes equally well with any grilled meat or seafood.

1½ cups Chicken Stock (page 28)

1 cup chopped onion

6 tablespoons (3 ounces) unsalted butter

1 cup instant couscous

½ cup golden raisins

1½ teaspoons kosher salt or more to taste

1½ cups toasted sliced almonds

¼ cup fresh lemon juice

⅓ cup minced fresh parsley

⅓ cup chopped fresh chives

⅓ cup chopped fresh mint leaves

In a small saucepan bring the chicken stock to a boil, lower the heat, and cover the pan to keep the stock hot. Sauté the onions in butter in a large saucepan over medium heat until onions are light brown. Add the couscous, raisins, salt, and the hot chicken stock. Stir to blend. Remove pan from heat, cover, and let stand for 8 to 10 minutes.

Add the almonds, lemon juice, parsley, chives, and mint and blend with a fork, fluffing the couscous to break up any lumps. If needed, add more salt or lemon juice. If the couscous seems dry, add more chicken stock or some olive oil. Let the couscous stand at room temperature until ready to be served.

Yields 4 to 6 servings

Toasted Israeli Couscous

Israeli couscous is a versatile pasta that absorbs liquids while remaining pleasantly al dente. This is a great side to serve with grilled lamb or beef.

1 tablespoon olive oil

1 clove garlic, minced

8 ounces Israeli couscous

2½ cups water

½ pound pencil-thin asparagus, trimmed, sliced into 1½-inch pieces, and blanched for 1 minute

1 bunch scallions, chopped fine (green part only)

1½ tablespoons finely chopped fresh mint leaves

⅔ cup raisins

Dressing

2 tablespoons fresh lemon juice

1 teaspoon Dijon mustard

3 tablespoons olive oil

1½ teaspoons kosher salt

¼ teaspoon cayenne pepper

Heat the olive oil in a heavy saucepan over medium heat. Add the garlic and couscous and sauté for 5 minutes. Add the water, stir once, and bring to a boil. Lower the heat, cover, and simmer for 10 minutes until the pasta is tender.

Place the couscous in a bowl. Add the asparagus, scallions, mint, and raisins.

To make the dressing, combine the lemon juice, mustard, olive oil, salt, and cayenne in a jar with a tight-fitting lid and shake well to blend. Pour the dressing over the couscous and toss to blend. Serve warm or at room temperature.

Yields 4 to 6 servings

Mesclun, Peaches, Pecans, and Goat Cheese Salad

We often have this beautiful, tasty salad as a main course, accompanied by crusty bread, chilled white wine or Champagne and, for dessert, a scoop or two of our favorite ice cream, with homemade cookies on the side.

8 cups mesclun salad mix

½ cup thinly sliced red onion

4 very ripe peaches, each sliced into 8 wedges

¾ cup toasted pecan halves

¼ cup peanut oil

12 ounces fresh goat cheese, shaped into 8 discs

2 egg whites, beaten

1 cup panko or dry bread crumbs

Dressing

2 tablespoons white wine vinegar

2 tablespoons walnut oil

2 tablespoons olive oil

1 teaspoon Dijon mustard

½ teaspoon kosher salt

½ teaspoon freshly ground black pepper

½ teaspoon sugar

Place the greens in a large bowl. Add the onion, peaches, and pecans.

Pour the peanut oil into a skillet and heat until very hot. Dip the goat cheese discs, one at a time, first into the egg whites, then into the panko. Place the breaded discs in the hot oil. Sauté just to brown, turning once. Transfer discs onto paper towels to drain.

To make the dressing, combine the vinegar, oils, mustard, salt, pepper, and sugar in a jar with a tight-fitting lid and shake well to blend. Pour over the salad and toss gently to blend. Arrange the salad on four dinner plates. Place 2 goat cheese rounds on top of greens and serve.

Yields 4 servings

Butter Beans, Tomatoes, and Olives in a Lemon Dressing

Butter beans are very large white, creamy, and delicious beans, sometimes called gigantes or white runners. They're almost impossible to find fresh. I am able to buy them picked and frozen in the South, but I prefer using dried beans, since they have a lot more flavor. This recipe should be prepared a day ahead since the beans need to soak overnight.

1 pound dried large white beans

¾ cup thinly sliced red onion

1 cup yellow cherry tomatoes, cut in half

1 cup red cherry tomatoes, cut in half

½ cup calamata olives, pitted and cut in half

1½ teaspoons grated lemon zest

Lemon Dressing

1 large clove garlic, minced

1 tablespoon kosher salt

2 teaspoons freshly ground black pepper

2½ tablespoons fresh lemon juice

½ cup olive oil

3 cups slightly bitter greens, such as mizuna, arugula, or flat-leaf parsley

Place the beans in a large pot, cover with 2 quarts cold water and let them soak overnight in the refrigerator.

Drain the beans, return them to the pot, cover with 2 quarts fresh cold water, and bring to a boil. Lower the heat and simmer for 1 hour or more, until tender. Drain and transfer the beans to a salad bowl.

Add the onions, tomatoes, olives, and lemon zest.

To make the dressing, mash the garlic and salt into a paste and add it to the beans. Add the pepper, lemon juice, and olive oil and toss to blend well. Let the salad stand at room temperature until serving time. Just before serving, toss the greens of your choice in with the beans.

Yields 8 servings

❊ Any leftover salad can be covered and stored in the refrigerator for up to 4 days.

❊ Much of the cooking time depends largely on the kind of bean you have chosen. It would be advisable, if the bean is smaller, to check for doneness sooner.

❊ If you cannot find gigante beans, substitute large dried lima beans or almost any dried bean you prefer.

Watermelon and Feta Cheese Salad

Here in the Hamptons the peak season for melon is August. This gorgeous, cool salad is an excellent way of combining sweet and savory with surprising effect.

One 3-pound piece watermelon, pits and rind removed, cut into ¾-inch cubes

3 tablespoons fresh lime juice

2 tablespoons olive oil

1 teaspoon sugar

½ teaspoon kosher salt

1 teaspoon freshly ground black pepper

6 ounces feta cheese, crumbled (about 1 cup)

½ cup packed fresh cilantro leaves

⅓ cup toasted pine nuts

Place the melon pieces in a bowl. In another bowl, whisk together the lime juice, oil, sugar, salt, and pepper. Pour dressing over melon. Toss gently to coat. Add the feta, cilantro, and pine nuts and toss just to blend. Serve chilled.

Yields 4 servings

✼ Variation: Add 1½ cups cubed tomatoes, fresh crumbled goat cheese, and chopped fresh mint leaves to the dressed melon cubes. And when you're in the mood for a bit of crunch, try substituting ⅓ cup toasted peanuts, cashews, or pecans for the pine nuts.

Black Mission Figs with Goat Cheese and Upland Cress

You can substitute watercress for the upland cress. Both have a similar peppery taste that gives this salad a lot of spunk.

1 teaspoon unsalted butter, softened

12 large black mission figs, halved, stems removed

4 ounces fresh goat cheese such as Caprino di Latte di Capra or Montrachet

¼ cup aged balsamic vinegar

1 tablespoon palm sugar or light brown sugar

¼ teaspoon kosher salt

¼ teaspoon freshly ground black pepper

1 basket upland cress or 2 bunches watercress

Preheat the oven to 400°F. Butter a 9-inch glass pie dish.

Place figs cut side up in the baking dish. Using a teaspoon, make an indentation in each fig half. Roast the figs for 15 minutes. Remove from oven and fill each indentation with goat cheese. Return to the oven and roast 5 minutes longer.

Warm the vinegar, sugar, salt, and pepper in a small saucepan. Stir until the sugar is dissolved.

Distribute the cress among four salad plates. Arrange 6 fig halves on each plate. Drizzle 1 tablespoon of the warmed vinegar mixture over the figs and cress and trickle some onto each plate.

Yields 4 servings

❧ This recipe can be doubled to serve 8.

Asparagus Salad with Roasted Peppers and Goat Cheese

I created this salad during a cooking demonstration at our local college and it turned out to be a great success, mostly because it features asparagus, which many people refer to as "King of the Vegetables."

2 tablespoons olive oil

2 large red bell peppers, quartered; seeds, stems, and cores removed and discarded

2 pounds medium asparagus, trimmed and peeled

8 ounces baby spinach, washed and thoroughly dried

½ red onion, thinly sliced

Dressing

1 clove garlic, finely chopped

3 tablespoons white wine vinegar

½ cup plus 2 tablespoons olive oil

Kosher salt and freshly ground black pepper to taste

½ cup pitted black olives, cut in half

6 ounces fresh mild goat cheese, crumbled (about 1 cup)

Place a skillet on a hot grill. Add the oil and peppers, skin side up. Lower the heat to medium and close the lid. Grill the peppers 20 to 25 minutes, turning them once to make sure they don't burn.

Remove the peppers from the heat and set aside. When cool enough to handle, cut them into strips.

Cook the asparagus in boiling salted water until just tender but still bright green. Drain and rinse under cold water for a few minutes. Drain on paper towels or clean dish towels until ready to use.

Place the spinach, onion, grilled pepper strips, and asparagus in a salad bowl.

Combine the garlic, vinegar, olive oil, salt, and pepper in a jar with a tight-fitting lid and shake well to blend. Spoon half the dressing over the salad. Mix gently to coat all the vegetables. Just before serving, sprinkle the salad with the olives and goat cheese. Offer any extra dressing on the side.

Yields 6 to 8 servings

Asian-Flavor Beef, Pepper, and Spinach Salad

Hearty, flavorful, and easy to prepare, this is a salad for all seasons that is very popular with our customers and friends. Serve it for lunch or as a light dinner with a knock-out dessert.

1½ pounds top round steak, 1¼ inches thick

¼ cup olive oil

Kosher salt and freshly ground black pepper to taste

1 red bell pepper

½ red onion, cut into paper-thin half-moon slices

1½ cups fresh cilantro leaves

Dressing

¼ cup olive oil

3 tablespoons soy sauce

1½ teaspoons toasted sesame oil

2 tablespoons rice vinegar

1 teaspoon red pepper flakes

1 teaspoon sugar

4 pocketless pita breads

4 cups loosely packed baby spinach leaves, well washed and dried

Preheat the grill to high. Rub the steak with the olive oil, salt, and pepper.

Place the steak on the grill. For medium rare, grill 6 to 8 minutes per side. When done, set aside to cool.

Cut the pepper in half, discard inner core and grill until lightly charred. Cool.

Slice the warm steak on the diagonal into bite-size pieces and place in a large bowl. Cut the pepper into thin strips and add to the steak. Add the onion and cilantro.

To make the dressing, combine the olive oil, soy sauce, sesame oil, vinegar, pepper flakes, and sugar in a jar with a tight-fitting lid and shake well to blend. Pour the dressing over the salad. Toss well to coat all the meat and vegetables.

Grill the pita bread until light brown. Place 1 bread round on each of four dinner plates. Top each round with a cup of spinach. Scoop beef salad onto each bed of spinach, distributing it equally among the plates.

Yields 4 main-course servings

Chicken in Basil Cream

Another customer favorite, straight from our kitchen. When doubled, this recipe could accommodate a larger group of 8.

2 large whole chicken breasts (about 2 pounds), skin and bones removed

½ red onion, sliced paper thin

½ cup finely chopped celery

1½ cups seedless green grapes, halved

Basil Cream

1 clove garlic, sliced

1½ cups loosely packed fresh basil leaves, rinsed and patted dry

2 tablespoons fresh lemon juice

1 cup mayonnaise

2 teaspoons kosher salt

1 teaspoon freshly ground black pepper

1 teaspoon sugar

1 small head red leaf lettuce, leaves separated, rinsed, and dried

Place the chicken breasts in a large saucepan, cover with cold water, and bring to a boil. Lower the heat and simmer for 12 to 15 minutes, depending on the thickness of the breasts. Drain and cool.

Cut the chicken into bite-size pieces and place in a large bowl. Add the onion, celery, and grapes.

For the basil cream: combine the garlic, basil, and lemon juice in a food processor or blender, and process until smooth. Add the mayonnaise, salt, pepper, and sugar, and pulse a few times to blend. Pour over the chicken and mix well, to coat all.

Distribute the lettuce among four serving plates. Top each with a scoop of the chicken in basil cream and serve.

Yields 4 servings

Spicy Chicken Salad with Lemon and Sesame Seeds

You'll find yourself making this throughout the summer. It has a nice bite and crunch and leftovers (if any!) make superb sandwiches.

1½ pounds chicken breasts, skin and bones removed

4 scallions, sliced thin (white and green parts)

½ cup chopped celery

½ cup red bell pepper, sliced into thin strips

½ cup yellow bell pepper, sliced into thin strips

1 cup julienne or shredded carrots

1 tablespoon minced seeded jalapeños (or less if preferred)

1 teaspoon grated lemon zest

1 tablespoon toasted sesame seeds

2 tablespoons chopped fresh cilantro

¾ cup broccoli cut into very small florets

Dressing

¼ cup olive oil

1 tablespoon fresh lemon juice

2 tablespoons rice vinegar

1 teaspoon toasted sesame oil

1 tablespoon Dijon mustard

1½ teaspoons kosher salt

1 teaspoon sugar

Bring 2 quarts of water to a rapid boil. Add the chicken, cover, and turn off heat. Let it stand for 2 hours. The chicken will be moist and just done.

Remove chicken from the pot. Cut into bite-size chunks and place in a mixing bowl. Add the scallions, celery, peppers, carrots, jalapeños, lemon zest, sesame seeds, cilantro, and broccoli.

Place all the ingredients for the dressing in a jar with a tight-fitting lid and shake well to blend. Pour it over the salad and toss gently to combine.

Yields 6 servings

Grilled Chicken Salad with Sugar Snap Peas and Arugula

This Asian-accented salad is one of the more popular take-out foods at Loaves and Fishes. Many customers refer to it as "Anna's Chicken Salad," but really, it isn't. Eight years ago, our daughter Sybille said, "Mom, we need a new chicken salad at the store," and this is what she created. We've made it every day since. It's been printed once before but here it is again by popular request.

3 pounds boneless chicken breasts, skin removed, cut in half

1 tablespoon toasted sesame oil

1½ tablespoons soy sauce

1 tablespoon fresh lemon juice

1 clove garlic, minced

½ teaspoon red pepper flakes

2 teaspoons Dijon mustard

¼ cup dry white wine

Dressing

1 clove garlic, minced

1 tablespoon toasted sesame oil

2 tablespoons soy sauce

2 tablespoons sherry vinegar

⅓ cup olive oil

½ teaspoon cayenne pepper

Salad

½ cup paper-thin sliced red onion

1½ cups sugar snap peas, trimmed

⅓ cup dried cranberries or pitted sour cherries

1 bunch fresh arugula or baby spinach leaves, well washed and dried

Heat the grill to high. Place the chicken in a shallow casserole. Whisk together the sesame oil, soy sauce, lemon juice, garlic, pepper flakes, mustard, and wine and pour it over the chicken. Set it aside for 20 minutes, at room temperature, to marinate.

Grill the chicken 8 to 10 minutes, turning once. Cut into bite-size strips and place in a salad bowl. Discard the marinade.

Purée all the dressing ingredients in a food processor until smooth. Pour over the chicken.

Add the onion, peas, and cranberries and toss to blend. Fold in the arugula. Serve at room temperature.

Yields 6 servings

Magret of Duck and Wild Rice Salad

The chewy texture of wild rice, the velvety texture of duck, the sweet crunch of sugar snap peas, and the tartness of dried cranberries, turns this into an excellent lunch or a light supper. Serve warm or at room temperature.

¾ cup wild rice

2 cups sugar snap peas, cut on the diagonal

6 scallions, sliced thin (green parts only)

Grated zest of 1 orange

½ cup dried cranberries

¼ cup finely chopped fresh mint

¼ cup finely chopped fresh parsley

1 clove garlic, mashed with 1 teaspoon kosher salt

Two 14-ounce boneless duck breasts, skin and fat removed

Kosher salt and freshly ground black pepper

2 tablespoons olive oil

1 cup pecan halves

3 ripe peaches, pitted, peeled, and cut into bite-size chunks

Dressing

4 tablespoons olive oil

2 tablespoons red wine vinegar

½ teaspoon hot pepper sauce

½ teaspoon sugar

½ teaspoon freshly ground black pepper

Cook the rice in 4 cups boiling water for 40 minutes or until tender. Drain well. Transfer to a salad bowl and add the sugar snap peas, scallions, orange zest, cranberries, mint, parsley, and garlic/salt mixture.

Season both sides of the duck breasts with salt and pepper.

Pour 2 tablespoons olive oil in a heavy skillet over high heat. When the oil is smoking hot, add the duck. Sauté for 5 minutes, turning once. Transfer duck to a cutting board.

Using the same skillet, sauté the pecans over high heat for 2 minutes, stirring constantly. Add the pecans to the rice.

Cut the duck across the grain into thin slices and add to the rice.

Combine all the dressing ingredients in a jar with a tight-fitting lid and shake well to blend. Pour the dressing over the salad and toss well to combine it all.

Gently fold the peach chunks into the salad. Serve.

Yields 6 main-course servings

Halibut Salad

When I bought Loaves and Fishes back in 1980, it was a small take-out food store. This is one of the prepared foods sold there at the time. The original recipe called for bluefish fillet. We like using either halibut or fresh tuna.

2 tablespoons olive oil

2 pounds halibut fillet

2 tablespoons fresh lemon juice

1 cup finely chopped celery

1 cup finely chopped red onion

⅓ cup finely chopped fresh dill

¼ cup capers, drained

⅓ cup distilled white vinegar

Grated zest of half a lime

¾ cup mayonnaise

2 teaspoons kosher salt

1 teaspoon freshly ground pepper

Preheat the oven to 400°F or set grill to medium-high. Brush a large sheet pan with the oil.

Cut the fish into 6 equal pieces and place on the sheet pan. Turn the pieces once to coat both sides with oil. Sprinkle the fish with some of the lemon juice and bake or grill for 15 minutes. Cool.

Place the halibut in a mixing bowl and, with your hands, break it into small pieces. Add the remaining lemon juice, celery, onion, dill, capers, vinegar, lime zest, mayonnaise, salt, and pepper and mix gently but thoroughly.

Yields 6 main-course servings, many more as a starter

❧ The Halibut Salad will last up to 3 days if covered and kept chilled in the refrigerator.

❧ As a fine starter, spoon the fish onto small, thin slices of toasted crostini and garnish with dill sprigs.

❧ As a salad, serve a generous portion on a bed of mixed greens, garnished with lemon wedges.

❧ Or, for a great sandwich, stuff the salad between slices of whole-wheat bread or in a soft kaiser roll. Add sprouts for some crunch.

Turkey, Peaches, Avocado, and Romaine Salad

No cooking involved! This is a dish that only requires assembling. A perfect, satisfying salad for an August lunch or brunch.

> 1½ pounds smoked turkey breast, sliced ½-inch thick
>
> 2 ripe peaches
>
> 2 navel oranges
>
> 2 ripe avocados
>
> ¼ cantaloupe
>
> 6 cups coarsely chopped romaine lettuce
>
> 6 scallions, chopped fine (white and green parts)
>
> 1 cup toasted cashews, coarsely chopped

Dressing

> ½ cup extra virgin olive oil
>
> ¼ cup white wine vinegar
>
> 2 teaspoons sugar
>
> 1 teaspoon Dijon mustard
>
> ½ teaspoon kosher salt
>
> ½ teaspoon freshly ground black pepper

Cut the turkey into 1½ x ¼-inch strips and place in a large bowl. Halve and pit the peaches, cut into bite-size pieces, and add to the turkey.

Peel and cut the oranges, avocados, and cantaloupe into bite-size pieces. Add to the turkey along with the romaine, scallions, and cashews.

Place dressing ingredients in a jar with a tight-fitting lid and shake well to blend. Pour the dressing over the salad and mix gently to coat, being sure not to bruise or mash the ingredients.

Yields more than 6 servings

Cold Lobster à la Loaves and Fishes

By unanimous popular demand—one of our very best. Double the ingredients for 8 servings.

1½ pounds chilled cooked lobster meat, cut in chunks

2 teaspoons fresh lemon juice

1 tablespoon capers, drained

½ cup mayonnaise

½ teaspoon kosher salt

½ teaspoon freshly ground black pepper

¼ cup finely chopped fresh dill

Place the lobster meat in a large bowl, add the lemon juice, capers, mayonnaise, salt, pepper, and dill and mix gently with your hands.

Yields 4 servings

❧ For a heartier salad, garnish with chopped red onions, chopped hard-boiled eggs, tomatoes, capers, and caviar.

❧ For a memorable first course, serve the lobster over fresh greens with a lemon wedge on the side and a sprinkling of caviar on top.

❧ For delightful hors d'oeuvres, spoon the lobster onto small pieces of crostini and pass them around.

❧ To make our famous lobster rolls, for a bit of crunch, add chopped celery and sugar snap peas, cut small and on the diagonal, and serve inside a fresh baguette.

Soft Polenta with Gorgonzola

Creamy Gorgonzola lends a special flavor to the polenta. A perfect side to grilled lamb, chicken or veal and it's super easy to prepare.

> 5 cups water
> 1 cup half-and-half
> 4 tablespoons (2 ounces) unsalted butter
> 4 ounces Gorgonzola cheese, crumbled
> 2 teaspoons kosher salt
> 1¼ cups instant polenta or fine cornmeal

Place the water, half and half, and butter in a large saucepan and bring to a boil. Add the Gorgonzola and salt. In a slow, steady stream, while stirring continually, pour the polenta into the boiling mixture. Lower the heat to medium and cook for about 5 minutes, continuing to stir throughout, until the polenta thickens. Turn off the heat. Cover the pan and let the polenta steam for 10 minutes. Serve hot.

Yields 4 to 6 servings

> ❋ If you prefer a lighter cheese with a subtler taste, replace the Gorgonzola with fresh goat cheese or grated Swiss or Gruyère.

Baked Tomatoes Filled with Pine Nuts and Garlic Crumbs

For a tasty and colorful first course, serve the Baked Tomatoes on some dressed baby arugula. This is a wonderful go-with for grilled pork or veal.

3 large summer tomatoes, cut in half crosswise

1 tablespoon olive oil

½ cup fresh bread crumbs

2 cloves garlic, minced

1 teaspoon fresh thyme leaves

2 tablespoons pine nuts

⅓ cup grated Parmesan cheese

1 teaspoon kosher salt

½ teaspoon freshly ground black pepper

Preheat the oven to 400°F.

Brush the tomato halves with olive oil and place cut side down in a large cast-iron skillet. Cook over high heat for 5 minutes, or until light brown. Remove pan from the heat. With a spatula, carefully turn tomatoes cut side up.

Place the bread crumbs, garlic, thyme, pine nuts, Parmesan, salt, and pepper in a bowl and mix to blend. Distribute the crumb mixture evenly over the top of the tomato halves. Bake 20 minutes. Serve hot.

Yields 6 servings

❦ This dish can be made earlier in the day and reheated.

Gratin of Potatoes, Tomatoes, and Tarragon

This is a perfect partner with grilled steak.

2½ pounds Yukon Gold or any other firm yellow
   potato
1 cup coarsely chopped onion
1 clove garlic, minced
2 tablespoons olive oil
1 tablespoon chopped fresh tarragon leaves
1½ pounds tomatoes, sliced
2 teaspoons kosher salt
½ teaspoon freshly ground black pepper
⅓ cup Chicken Stock (page 28)
⅓ cup olive oil
1½ cups grated Swiss cheese

Cut potatoes in half, place in a large saucepan, cover with water, and bring to a boil. Lower the heat and cook 15 minutes until potatoes feel tender. Drain and cool. When cool enough to handle, peel and slice the potatoes and set aside.

Place a skillet over medium heat, add the olive oil, and sauté the onion and garlic, stirring often, for 10 minutes. Stir in the tarragon.

Butter a 2-quart metal casserole. Heat the grill to medium.

Layer the bottom of the casserole with half the potatoes. Cover that with a layer of sliced tomatoes and sprinkle with half of the salt and pepper. Spread the onion-tarragon mixture over it all. Place the final layer of potatoes on top and season with the remaining salt and pepper. Drizzle chicken stock and olive oil over the potatoes and top with cheese. Place the casserole on the grill, close the lid, and bake for 30 minutes. Serve hot.

Yields 6 servings

❧ To bake, preheat the oven to 375°F and bake the casserole for 30 minutes.

❧ I know the instructions say to close the grill lid, but the casserole itself, inside the grill *or* the oven, should not be covered. If it is, the cheese will not crisp or brown and the casserole will not cook properly.

Sauté of Spinach with Sesame Seeds and Lemon

For cooked spinach dishes, I use the curly large-leaf kind. It has lots of flavor and maintains its texture. This recipe can easily be doubled to serve 8.

2 tablespoons olive oil

1 tablespoon sesame seeds

1½ pounds fresh spinach, stemmed, washed well, and coarsely chopped

1 tablespoon fresh lemon juice

2 teaspoons soy sauce

½ teaspoon freshly ground black pepper

Heat the olive oil in a large saucepan, add the sesame seeds, and stir over medium heat until seeds turn light brown and fragrant. Add the spinach all at once, cover, and cook for 1 minute. Add the lemon juice, soy sauce, and pepper. Cook 1 minute longer, turning with tongs, until the spinach is wilted. Serve warm, set aside and reheat when needed.

Yields 4 servings

Grilled Shallots and Grape Tomatoes with Fresh Basil

Excellent with grilled chicken or steaks.

> 1¼ pounds (4 cups) medium shallots, quartered lengthwise
>
> ¼ cup olive oil
>
> 2 tablespoons balsamic vinegar
>
> 1 teaspoon kosher salt
>
> ½ teaspoon freshly ground black pepper
>
> ½ teaspoon sugar
>
> 10 ounces red grape tomatoes
>
> ½ cup fresh basil leaves, coarsely chopped

Preheat the grill to medium-high.

Combine the shallots, olive oil, vinegar, salt, pepper, and sugar in a shallow roasting pan. Stir thoroughly, making sure all the shallots are coated. Set the pan on the grill, close the cover, and grill 12 to 15 minutes, stirring once or twice, until shallots are crisp-tender. Add the grape tomatoes and, without disturbing them, grill 5 minutes. Transfer to a serving dish and garnish with the basil.

Yields 4 to 6 servings

✺ If using the oven, preheat the oven to 500°F and bake 12 to 15 minutes.

✺ If you can't find shallots, small red onions are a fine substitute.

GRILLING VEGETABLES

There are numerous herbs you could mince and sprinkle onto vegetables, or use Herb-Infused Oil (page 3) to coat vegetables before baking or grilling. I love my Microplane grater—it's another way to deal with garlic without having to mash it by hand. I add the Microplaned garlic to oil, along with salt and pepper and toss it thoroughly with the vegetables before grilling or baking.

A word of caution: I suggest that you keep a watchful eye on grilling vegetables to make sure they don't burn or are too undercooked. If it seems as if they are cooking too rapidly, move them to a cooler portion of the grill where there is less direct heat.

Here is a variety of vegetables that you may choose as go-withs for your main dish. Now is the time to experiment!

Eggplant

Cut into ½-inch-thick rounds. Coat with oil, kosher salt, and pepper. Bake 30 minutes at 400°F or grill at medium-high heat for 15 minutes, turning once to brown both sides.

Zucchini

Cut on the diagonal into long ¾-inch-thick slices. Brush with olive oil, sprinkle with kosher salt. Grill 12 to 15 minutes, turning once.

Peppers

Cut into strips or quarters. Coat with oil, kosher salt, and pepper. Bake at 400°F for 30 minutes or grill 12 to 15 minutes on medium-high heat, turning them once.

Onions

Slice ¼-inch thick. Coat with oil, kosher salt, and pepper. Bake 30 minutes at 400°F or grill on medium-high heat for 15 minutes, turning once.

Potatoes

Slice into rounds or sticks and coat with oil, kosher salt, and pepper. Bake at 400°F for 30 minutes or grill at medium-high heat for 30 minutes, turning once or twice to brown evenly.

Broccoli, Cauliflower, and Brussels Sprouts

Toss with a mixture of olive oil, garlic (optional), kosher salt, and pepper. Bake at 400°F for 30 to 40 minutes or grill at medium-high heat for 15 to 20 minutes, depending on your desired crispness.

Corn on the Cob

Husk the corn and remove the silk. The corn could be buttered or coated with olive oil, kosher salt, and pepper, and Microplaned garlic if you like. Place on grill at medium-high heat. It doesn't need much cooking time; turn, watching until the ears are browned in spots all around the corn.

Grilled Green Asparagus

2 pounds medium green asparagus, peeled and trimmed

3 tablespoons olive oil

1 teaspoon kosher salt

½ teaspoon freshly ground black pepper

⅓ cup grated Parmesan cheese

Preheat the grill to high.

Arrange the asparagus spears in a single layer inside a metal roasting pan. Drizzle with olive oil and season with salt and pepper. Using your hands, roll asparagus around, making sure all spears are coated. Sprinkle with Parmesan cheese and place the pan on the hot grill. With lid closed, grill asparagus 5 to 8 minutes, until crisp tender.

Yields 4 servings

✻ This recipe can be doubled. If using an oven, preheat to 400°F, prepare the asparagus as directed for grilling, and bake for 15 minutes.

Grilled Sweet Potato Fries

4 medium sweet potatoes or yams, washed and cut lengthwise into ½-inch-
thick sticks

1 teaspoon kosher salt

3 tablespoons extra virgin olive oil

Drop potato sticks into a bowl of cold water to rinse off starch. Dry on paper towels.

Pile potato sticks on a large baking sheet, add the salt and olive oil. Using your hands, toss strips with the mixture, making sure to coat evenly. Spread sticks across the pan.

Preheat the grill to medium. Place the baking sheet on the grill and close the cover. After 15 minutes, using a wide spatula, carefully turn the fries over. The total grilling time should be 30 minutes from start to finish.

Yields 4 servings

❋ For oven users: preheat the oven to 450°F. Spread the cut potatoes across the baking sheet and place in the oven. Roast the potatoes, turning fries once and rotating the sheet once during roasting time. In 45 to 50 minutes they ought to be nicely browned and crisp.

The Grill

When marketing for chops or steaks to grill, ask for cuts no less than 1½ inches thick. I found that when meats are only an inch thick, they cook too quickly and do not have enough time to develop those characteristic grid marks that are traditionally associated with grilled foods. Everyone expects to see those grid marks, and that additional half-inch makes a big difference. Also, please use tongs to turn meat. Forks are great but when they pierce the meat it allows those delicious juices to run out—juices that are essential to keeping the meat moist and tender.

The Big Outdoor Grill—My New Best Friend

As you have probably guessed by now, summer is my *favorite* season. It is when Loaves and Fishes is in high gear, positively bustling with activity, when our substantial daily output borders on "the impossible made to look simple." The number of recipes I have managed to accumulate over the years is mind-boggling. A major reason, besides its being the nature of my work, is that our Loaves and Fishes menu changes each and every week. Many of the newer recipes I credit to my most recent acquisition—a wonderful, multitasking, easy to maintain, cook-friendly outdoor grill.

Having been born on a working farm in Northern Germany, with many farm-hands and a rather large family to feed, I can only imagine now how much my dear mother, would have *adored* an outdoor grill. Oh my, when I think of how her life would have changed. As it happened, every summer we would move our large kitchen table into the garden, cover it with an oilcloth, our feet shaping a well-worn path as we raced back and forth from kitchen to garden, carting large platters of Mother's hot dishes, her homemade sausages and breads, fresh salads made from vegetables picked that morning, desserts—oh, the *desserts* and wheels of homemade aged cheese. The heat generated in the kitchen from my mother's daily output became really intense at times and so all of us would more than welcome every chance to enjoy the cooling relief provided by the occasional ocean or bay breeze that would drift our way. In the evening, especially when we had guests, the oilcloth was replaced by a starched linen tablecloth and napkins and our dinners would immediately take on a more elegant tone. Faces were illuminated by candlelight, music from my mother's tiny radio spilled outside from the kitchen and mingled with the hum of conversation—everyone contented, appreciative, chatting, laughing. There was an owl that always joined in, hooting from its roost inside one of the barns.

It was only about two, or maybe three years ago, when our daughter Sybille generously gifted us with a gorgeous outdoor grill. She and her husband own and operate a fabulous store in Bridgehampton where they sell top-quality cooking equipment and kitchen essentials. She knew exactly what would suit me best and, suddenly, there it was, waiting when I returned home from the store one evening. Honestly, I behaved like a child with a new toy. It wasn't as if I hadn't used one before, but those were catering grills, large and impersonal, necessary for cooking on a grand scale for parties of 100 or more. This grill was just the right size, and fit onto our patio perfectly. I became obsessed with this shiny new addition to our family and started to experiment and, ultimately, began to appreciate the finer points of grilling at home. Having a lid meant that I could roast whole chickens just as with my indoor oven. Grilling for a smaller crowd was a pure delight. The grill was placed near enough to the picnic table so I would be accessible, and most important—part of the dinner party. Slicing, dicing, shucking, many times I had my friends' elbows edging closer, lending a hand; not that I needed help, but it was the company that the grill invited. Friends asked me to explain why one cut of meat was better than such and such, how long did I cook this or that, what is that condiment, what is *in* that sauce?

During the second season of enjoying our wonderful grill, I thought how wonderful it would be to grill some duck breasts for our company that evening. The guests arrived, the grill was heated, the duck breasts were plump, fatty, and seasoned. On the grill they went and within seconds, the duck fat ignited and we experienced a flare-up so enormous that Detlef had to summon the local fire department. Luckily they didn't have to turn on the hoses, since the fire had died down by the time they arrived. I was embarrassed, yes, but more concerned that our wonderful grill wasn't damaged.

When we opened the lid, there they were, eight pathetic charred and shriveled duck breasts. I put them aside, thinking they were unsalvageable, but Sybille, curious, cut into one; the meat under the charred crust looked absolutely fine. She scraped off some of the blackened skin, put a bite into her mouth and her eyes immediately widened in surprise. "This is absolutely . . . *delicious!*" she said. No, we didn't eat them, but the whole experience turned out to be an eye-opening lesson.

The next day I did a thorough check-through of my grilling paraphernalia. I'm suggesting you do the same. Search through your utensils and tools, update old ones, throw away any that almost work but really don't. The fork with the loose handle you think might last one more season? Throw it away. Proper "to-the-elbow" gloves, those handy long-handled basting brushes, a thermometer for the grill and an instant-read for the meats; tongs, and, oh, yes, drip pans to avoid flare-ups. The cumulative lessons I have learned were gradual and gained through experience. Now it's clear sailing.

Perfect Grilled Whole Chicken with Plum Chutney

There is nothing better than a well-cooked and beautifully presented grilled chicken, served with chutney, grilled corn, and perhaps a fresh spinach salad. It is my idea of an idyllic Sunday dinner. I suggest you make the Plum Chutney first since it takes longer to cook and needs time to cool to room temperature.

Plum Chutney

1½ pounds fresh prune plums, pitted and sliced thin

½ cup peeled and minced fresh ginger

½ cup finely chopped onion

¼ cup pitted prunes, chopped fine

2 cups apple cider vinegar

1⅔ packed cups light brown sugar

1 tablespoon Dijon mustard

1½ teaspoons kosher salt

Chicken

3 cloves garlic, minced

1 cup finely chopped onion

1 lemon, all pits removed but rind left on, finely chopped

1 tablespoon chopped fresh tarragon leaves

Two 3-pound chickens, rinsed and patted dry

The rub

2 teaspoons kosher salt

½ teaspoon cayenne pepper

3 tablespoons olive oil

Juice of 1 lemon (about 2½ tablespoons)

To make the chutney, combine all the ingredients in a large heavy saucepan and bring to a boil. Lower the heat and stirring often, continue to cook the chutney, uncovered, for 1 to 1½ hours, until it begins to thicken. Take care not to let it boil or burn. When thickened, spoon the chutney into a bowl or glass jars and allow it to cool to room temperature.

Preheat the grill to 400°F. Make sure your oven thermometer is inside the grill. For ideal results it is essential to maintain a constant temperature throughout the grilling time.

Mix together the garlic, onion, lemon, and tarragon in a small bowl. Split the mixture, stuff half of it into the cavity of each chicken. Tie the legs together with kitchen string to keep stuffing inside the bird.

To make the rub, whisk together the salt, cayenne, oil, and lemon juice in a small bowl and rub this mixture over the chickens, making sure to coat all sides well. Place the chickens, side by side, breast side down, in a grill pan.

Grill the chickens with the lid closed, at 400°F for 40 minutes. After the first 10 minutes, check the temperature. The roasting temperature must remain at 400°F throughout the entire roasting time. After 40 minutes, turn the chickens on their backs and grill 40 minutes longer. Test for doneness by inserting an instant-read thermometer into the thigh, not touching the bone. It should read 165°F. Transfer chickens to a platter and cut into serving-size pieces. Serve the plum chutney on the side.

Yields 4 to 6 servings

❧ You can substitute fresh peaches or apricots for the plums. They make really nice chutneys, each with a distinct flavor. Covered and stored in the refrigerator, they will last up to 4 weeks and are tasty sides to serve with any poultry or pork dish. Also, they are delicious on sandwiches of ham, turkey, or chicken.

❧ The Plum Chutney could be made the day before and chilled until ready to serve.

Grilled Boneless Chicken Breasts with Tarragon-Mustard Butter

The Tarragon-Mustard Butter should be made the day before, wrapped and refrigerated, giving the flavors time to blend. Grilled summer squash and grilled bread will round out this meal beautifully.

Tarragon-Mustard Butter

16 tablespoons (8 ounces) unsalted butter, softened

2 teaspoons fresh lemon juice

1 tablespoon Dijon mustard

½ teaspoon hot pepper sauce

½ teaspoon kosher salt

1½ tablespoons finely chopped fresh tarragon

4 boneless, skinless chicken breast halves, about 2 pounds

2 tablespoons fresh lemon juice

2 tablespoons dry white wine

¼ cup olive oil

2 tablespoons honey

½ teaspoon red pepper flakes

1 teaspoon kosher salt

Fresh tarragon sprigs, for garnish

To make the tarragon-mustard butter, combine the butter, lemon juice, mustard, hot sauce, salt, and tarragon in a small bowl and stir until smooth.

Place a piece of plastic wrap on your work surface. Scrape the butter onto it and roll to shape into a short roll. Twist each end of plastic wrap to seal it. Refrigerate overnight, if possible.

Butterfly the chicken breasts by slitting each horizontally down the center, but not all the way through, so that each piece opens like a book. Place the chicken pieces in a shallow casserole. In a bowl, whisk together the lemon juice, wine, olive oil, honey, pepper flakes, and salt. Pour it over the chicken. Turn and rub the mixture into the chicken to coat. Let it stand at room temperature for 20 minutes. Meanwhile preheat the grill to very hot.

Lay the chicken on the hot grill. Cook covered for 5 minutes. Turn, cover and cook 4 to 5 minutes longer, or until just cooked through.

To serve, place the hot grilled chicken on a platter. Cut tarragon-mustard butter into ⅓-inch slices and lay these over the chicken, allowing the butter to melt into a flavorful sauce.

Yields 4 servings

❋ Substitute basil or cilantro for the tarragon in the butter and take this chicken dish into a whole new flavor direction.

Parmesan-Panko Crusted Chicken with Black Bean–Avocado Salsa

A wonderful recipe that is full of possibilities as a main course. Sliced, it creates delicious sandwiches for picnics on the beach.

3 large chicken breasts, skinned, boned, halved, and butterflied

3 tablespoons peanut oil

½ cup mayonnaise

¼ cup Dijon mustard

1½ tablespoons honey

1½ cups panko or dry bread crumbs

2 teaspoons kosher salt

1 teaspoon freshly ground black pepper

1 cup grated Parmesan cheese

Salsa

1¾ cups cooked black beans or a 15-ounce can black beans, drained

1 ripe mango, peeled, pitted, and coarsely chopped

1 avocado, peeled, pitted, and coarsely chopped

1 cup finely chopped seedless cucumber, skin left on

½ cup finely chopped red onion

¼ cup fresh lime juice

1 tablespoon white wine vinegar

3 tablespoons olive oil

2 teaspoons hot pepper sauce

1 teaspoon kosher salt

1½ teaspoons sugar

⅓ cup chopped fresh cilantro

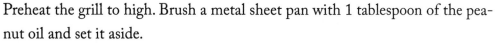
Preheat the grill to high. Brush a metal sheet pan with 1 tablespoon of the peanut oil and set it aside.

Combine the mayonnaise, mustard, and honey in a small bowl. Mix together the panko, salt, pepper, and Parmesan on a large sheet pan. Cover both sides of the chicken breasts, first with the mayonnaise mixture, then generously coat each breast with the panko mixture. Place the chicken on the oiled sheet pan and drizzle with the remaining peanut oil. Grill 20 minutes, turning once.

To make the salsa, combine all the ingredients in a bowl, stir well, and serve with the crispy chicken breasts.

Yields 4 to 6 servings

   ❧ For oven users: preheat oven to 500°F and follow the same directions as for grilling.

Grilled Pork Chops with Fruit Salsa

Brining the chops makes them succulent and juicy. The chops need to brine for 45 minutes and the salsa ought to chill for an hour.

½ cup kosher salt
½ cup sugar
1½ quarts cold water
Four 1½-inch-thick lean pork chops

Fruit Salsa

2 ripe peaches, pitted, and chopped
1 avocado, peeled, pitted, and chopped
1 ripe mango, peeled, pitted, and chopped
¼ cup minced shallots
½ red bell pepper, chopped
½ jalapeño pepper, seeded and minced
1 teaspoon kosher salt
2 tablespoons fresh lemon juice
1 tablespoon white wine vinegar
⅓ cup coarsely chopped fresh mint leaves

¼ cup olive oil
¼ cup coarsely ground black pepper
2 teaspoons fresh thyme leaves
2 teaspoons kosher salt

Dissolve the salt and sugar in the cold water to make the brine. Place the chops in a shallow casserole. Pour the brine over the meat and set it aside at room temperature for 45 minutes.

To make the salsa: combine all the ingredients in a bowl, and toss gently so as not to break up the fruit. Chill 1 hour to allow the juices to blend.

Preheat the grill to medium-high. Remove the chops from the brine and dry with paper towels. Combine the olive oil, pepper, thyme, and salt. Rub the mixture into the chops, on both sides. Grill, cover closed, 10 minutes per side. An instant-read thermometer should read 150°F to 155°F for just cooked. Serve the pork chops hot, with the chilled fruit salsa on the side.

Yields 4 servings

≉ This recipe can be doubled to serve 8.

≉ Lean pork can be a bit dry. Curing meat in a salt water solution makes it juicy and tender. Where I grew up on a farm in the most northern region of Germany, we butchered our own pigs. If my memory serves me correctly, there was a huge square free-form concrete basin in our cellar, where fresh hams, shoulder and loin meats were cured in a solution of cold water, salt, sugar, and saltpeter (potassium nitrate). We turned the meat every other day for 3 weeks. After that the meat was wrapped up in large kitchen towels and sent to the local smokehouse.

Grilled Pork Tenderloin with Rhubarb Sauce

As summer approaches the rhubarb in my garden seems to experience a sudden growth spurt, rising 14 to 16 inches high and begging to be eaten. This chilled sweet-and-sour sauce complements the grilled pork beautifully. Ideally, the rhubarb sauce should be made a day or two ahead to give the flavors a chance to blend. But it is still utterly delicious when chilled through, on the same day.

2 pounds rhubarb (about 6 cups) cut into 1-inch pieces

1 cup sugar

¼ cup honey

½ cup water

3 pounds pork tenderloin

1 tablespoon rubbed (ground) sage

2 teaspoons ground fennel

1 tablespoon kosher salt

1 teaspoon cayenne pepper

1 tablespoon Dijon mustard

⅓ cup olive oil

1 bunch watercress, rinsed and dried, stems removed

For the rhubarb sauce, place the rhubarb, sugar, honey, and water in a heavy saucepan and bring to a boil. Stir to blend, lower the heat, and simmer, covered, for 15 to 20 minutes until the rhubarb is tender. Transfer the rhubarb to a serving bowl and chill.

Trim the pork of all fat and sinew. Mash the sage, fennel, salt, pepper, mustard, and olive oil into a paste and rub the mixture over the tenderloin. Place the meat on a sheet pan and leave at room temperature for 30 minutes to marinate.

Preheat grill to medium-high.

Grill the pork for about 20 minutes, turning on all sides to brown evenly. Test for doneness by inserting an instant-read thermometer into the thickest part; it should read 150° to 155°F. Remove from the heat and allow 5 minutes for the juices to settle. The meat will be tender and juicy.

Slice and serve on a bed of watercress with chilled rhubarb sauce on the side.

Yields 6 servings

Barbecued Spareribs and Corn on the Cob

My family and I were invited to a potluck picnic, sponsored by the local church where we had just moved. It was the first American barbecue we had ever attended, celebrating the Fourth of July, 1960. I made a large potato salad with chopped scallions, parsley, salt, and pepper, and dressed it with a light vinaigrette. It was placed on one of the long picnic tables where there sat an abundance of glorious foods—spareribs, baked beans, coleslaw, watermelon, homemade fruit pies. It was a dazzling display of food, most of which we had never seen or tasted before. When anyone tasted my potato salad they all remarked, "What? No mayonnaise?" It was a blissful day of tasting, testing, and exchanging recipes. I have cooked this dish ever since and our family relishes it still.

> 3 racks of baby back pork ribs
> 2 teaspoons kosher salt
> 1 teaspoon freshly ground black pepper

Barbecue Sauce

> ¼ cup olive oil
> 2 cups finely chopped onion
> 4 cloves garlic, minced
> 4 cups canned crushed tomatoes with juices
> 1½ cups cider vinegar
> 1 cup red wine
> ½ cup molasses
> ½ cup light brown sugar
> 1 tablespoon Dijon mustard
> ¼ cup Worcestershire sauce
> 2 teaspoons red pepper flakes
> 1 teaspoon chili powder
> Zest of 1 orange, in strips
> 1 bay leaf

12 ears of fresh corn

12 tablespoons (6 ounces) melted unsalted butter or olive oil

1 clove garlic, minced

Preheat the oven to 350°F. Place ribs in a large roasting pan and sprinkle with 2 teaspoons salt and 1 teaspoon black pepper. Add 4 cups of water to the pan. Cover tightly with foil and roast the ribs for 2½ hours.

Remove foil. Cool 30 minutes or up to 3 hours.

For the barbecue sauce, place all the ingredients in a large heavy saucepan and bring to a boil. Lower the heat and simmer for 30 minutes, stirring often to keep sauce from burning. Remove from heat. Discard the orange zest and bay leaf. Set it aside.

Preheat the grill to medium-high.

Arrange the ribs on the grill and heat until lightly charred. Brush generously with the sauce, making sure every part is covered. Grill until the sauce is lightly charred. Turn the ribs carefully and brush with more sauce. Grill until charred on both sides. Total grilling time should be anywhere from 10 to 14 minutes, depending on your grill.

Cut the racks between bones, each into four pieces. Arrange the ribs on a platter and serve with sauce on the side.

Combine the melted butter with the garlic.

Remove the husks from the corn and brush lightly with the melted butter. Grill, turning a few times, until brown in spots on all sides.

Yields 6 servings, including 2 quarts sauce

- The ribs need little time on the grill. They have been precooked and must only heat, char, and absorb the sauce.

- Freeze extra sauce and save for your next cookout.

Marinated Butterflied Leg of Lamb

I enthusiastically recommend this for those summer dinners when daylight lasts until well past nine, the red wine is special, the dessert is yet to come, and no one wants to leave. So simple to prepare and so beautiful to present, this special dish transforms summer dinners into exceptional occasions.

One 7-pound leg of lamb, boned, trimmed of all fat, and butterflied (about 4
  pounds meat)
8 cloves garlic
1 cup honey
⅔ cup soy sauce
¼ cup olive oil
2 tablespoons fresh lemon juice
1 tablespoon chopped fresh rosemary, leaves only
1 teaspoon red pepper flakes

Place the lamb in a shallow casserole. Combine the garlic, honey, soy sauce, olive oil, lemon juice, rosemary, and pepper flakes in a food processor and process for 20 seconds. Pour the marinade over the lamb and let it sit at room temperature for 30 minutes, turning the lamb occasionally.

Preheat the grill to high.

Using paper towels, lightly pat the lamb dry. Reserve the marinade. Lower the heat a little and grill the lamb, 8 to 10 minutes per side. To check for doneness, insert an instant-read thermometer into the thickest part of the meat. It should read 130°F for medium rare. Transfer the lamb to a cutting board. Allow 5 minutes for the juices to settle.

Pour the marinade into a small saucepan and bring to a boil. Slice the lamb and serve with warm marinade on the side.

Yields 6 to 8 servings

⚘ If you don't have the means or time, ask your butcher to bone, trim, and butterfly the leg of lamb.

Grilled Loin Lamb Chops with Mint Hollandaise

The marinade is sweet and savory and when the intense heat of the grill seals in the juices it also helps to create a flavorful crust.

8 loin lamb chops, 1½ inches thick

3 cloves garlic

1 teaspoon kosher salt

1 teaspoon freshly ground black pepper

1 tablespoon minced fresh rosemary

2 tablespoons Dijon mustard

½ cup balsamic vinegar

2 tablespoons honey

Mint Hollandaise

⅓ cup fresh mint leaves, loosely packed

¼ cup fresh lemon juice

4 egg yolks

½ teaspoon freshly ground black pepper

½ teaspoon kosher salt

16 tablespoons (8 ounces) unsalted butter, melted

Fresh rosemary sprigs, for garnish

Place the lamb chops in a roasting pan. Crush the garlic, salt, and pepper together and place in a small bowl. Add the rosemary, mustard, vinegar, and honey and mash it all into a paste.

Spread paste over both sides of the chops. Set the chops aside for 30 minutes, to marinate at room temperature. Meanwhile, heat the grill to hot.

To make the mint hollandaise, blend the mint leaves and lemon juice at high speed for about 3 seconds. Add the egg yolks, pepper, and salt and blend for only a second. Then with the motor running, add the melted butter in a slow stream and blend for 2 seconds. Pour the Mint Hollandaise into a sauceboat and keep warm.

Grill the chops 8 to 10 minutes total for rare to medium-rare. Using tongs, so as not to pierce the flesh, turn once to brown on both sides. Transfer chops to a serving platter.

Place the roasting pan with leftover marinade on the grill, just to heat. Pour the hot marinade over the chops. Serve garnished with fresh rosemary sprigs and the mint hollandaise on the side.

Yields 4 servings

* This recipe can be doubled.

Grilled Sirloin Kebabs with Romaine-Parmigiana Salad

This is one of those satisfying summer meals you dream of in the middle of winter. To round everything out, add a simple baked potato topped with sour cream and croutons for the salad or olive oil–brushed grilled bread.

2 cloves garlic, minced

3 tablespoons red wine vinegar

3 tablespoons olive oil

1 teaspoon hot pepper flakes

1½ pounds boneless sirloin steak, 1½ inches thick, cut into 1½- to 2-inch cubes

12 cremini or white button mushrooms

2 red onions, cut into 1½-inch chunks

2 small heads romaine lettuce, torn into bite-size pieces

⅓ cup grated Parmesan cheese

Dressing

1 clove garlic, minced

1 flat anchovy fillet, minced

2 tablespoons fresh lemon juice

¼ cup olive oil

1 egg yolk

1 teaspoon Dijon mustard

2 tablespoons heavy cream

½ teaspoon freshly ground black pepper

Place the garlic, vinegar, oil, and pepper flakes in a medium bowl and whisk to blend. Add the beef cubes, mushrooms, and onion and set it aside at room temperature for 30 minutes to marinate. Preheat grill to high heat.

Skewer the meat and vegetables, alternating each, onto 12-inch-long metal skewers. Reserve the marinade. Place the kebabs on the grill for 12 to 14 minutes, depending on desired doneness, turning to brown kebabs on all sides.

Push meat and vegetables off the skewers onto four dinner plates.

Heat the marinade in a small pot on the grill and spoon it over the meat.

Place the romaine and Parmesan in a large bowl.

Combine the dressing ingredients in a jar with a tight-fitting lid and shake well to blend. Pour over the salad and toss well. Adjust seasoning, adding salt and pepper to taste. Distribute the salad next to the kebabs on each of the plates.

Yields 4 servings

Grilled Pepper Steak with Green Peppercorn Sauce

This classic French-style steak dinner is delicious, easy to prepare, and absolutely perfect for a special gathering.

Sauce

4 tablespoons (2 ounces) unsalted butter

2 shallots, finely chopped (about ⅓ cup)

¼ cup green peppercorns, drained and crushed

1 cup Chicken Stock (page 28)

½ cup dry white wine

1⅓ cups heavy cream

Kosher salt and freshly ground black pepper to taste

¼ cup minced flat-leaf parsley

4 New York strip steaks, 1½ inches thick (about 2½ pounds)

3 tablespoons coarsely cracked pepper

2 teaspoons kosher salt

¼ cup olive oil

Preheat the grill to high.

Melt the butter in a medium saucepan. Add the shallots and peppercorns. Cook over medium heat for 5 minutes, until the shallots turn glossy. Add the chicken stock and wine and bring to a boil. Continue cooking until the liquid has been reduced by half. Add the heavy cream, and salt and pepper to taste. Cook 5 minutes over medium-high heat, until the sauce coats a spoon. Set it aside at room temperature.

Season the steaks with the cracked pepper and salt. Brush the meat on both sides with the olive oil. Grill the steaks 4 to 5 minutes per side, turning to brown evenly. Transfer to four warmed dinner plates.

Reheat the sauce on the grill. Add the minced parsley. Nap the steaks with sauce and serve. Any remaining sauce can be passed around at serving time.

Yields 4 servings

❈ The sauce can be made up to 2 hours ahead. This recipe can be doubled.

Grilled Tenderloin of Beef with Fresh Herb Sauce

Grilling a whole beef filet is much easier than it seems and never fails to impress the guests. The beef marinates two hours before grilling, at which time the sauce can be prepared. The rest is as easy as one-two-three.

1 whole 6½- to 7-pound beef tenderloin (about 3½ pounds after trimming)

1 tablespoon sweet paprika

½ teaspoon cayenne pepper

1 tablespoon freshly ground black pepper

1 teaspoon ground coriander

1 teaspoon ground fennel

2 cloves garlic and 1 tablespoon kosher salt, mashed into a paste

⅓ cup olive oil

Herb Sauce

4 large cloves garlic

½ fresh jalapeño pepper, seeded and minced

3 tablespoons sherry vinegar

½ teaspoon kosher salt

½ teaspoon sugar

¾ cup chopped curly parsley, packed

½ cup chopped fresh cilantro

½ cup chopped fresh mint leaves, packed

1 cup olive oil

Fresh herb sprigs, for garnish

Two hours before grilling, place the beef tenderloin on a large sheet pan. Mix together the paprika, cayenne, pepper, coriander, fennel, garlic paste, and oil and rub the mixture over and into the beef tenderloin. Set it aside at room temperature to marinate.

To make the herb sauce, place the garlic and jalapeño in a food processor fitted with a metal blade and process for 30 seconds. Add the vinegar, salt, sugar, parsley, cilantro, mint, and oil and process until smooth. Pour the sauce into a bowl and set aside.

Preheat grill to high. Place the tenderloin on the hot grill. The meat should cook for 18 to 20 minutes in total; turn once. Insert an instant-read thermometer into the thickest part of the beef. It should read 120° to 125°F. If not, grill 3 to 4 minutes longer.

Transfer the meat to a cutting board, tent with foil and let it rest for 10 minutes, allowing time for the juices to settle.

Carve into ½-inch-thick slices. Garnish the platter with fresh herbs and serve tenderloin with herb sauce on the side.

Yields 6 to 8 servings

⁂ If using the oven, preheat it to 500°F. Roast the tenderloin for 22 minutes, remove from oven, and tent it with foil for 10 minutes. Uncover, slice, and enjoy.

Grilled Tri-Tip Steak with Tomato-Oregano Sauce

This cut of beef is shaped like a triangle and can be found in most butcher shops. It is well marbled with a texture much like flank steak, which means it soaks up marinade really well and is very tender.

Marinade

½ cup olive oil

¼ cup fresh lime juice

1 tablespoon grated lime zest

¼ cup soy sauce

¼ cup brandy

4 cloves garlic, smashed with 1 tablespoon kosher salt

2 teaspoons ground cumin

½ cup chopped fresh oregano

1 teaspoon dried oregano

1 teaspoon freshly ground black pepper

3 pounds trimmed tri-tip steak, cut into 6 pieces

Sauce

½ cup olive oil

¼ cup red wine vinegar

½ cup minced red onion

¼ cup minced mild chile peppers

1 teaspoon seeded and minced jalapeño pepper

4 cups teardrop or cherry tomatoes, halved

1 bunch fresh chives, chopped fine

1 small bunch fresh oregano, leaves only, chopped fine

1 teaspoon kosher salt

Combine the marinade ingredients in a food processor fitted with a metal blade and process until smooth. Place the steaks in a shallow casserole and pour the marinade over the meat. Let it rest at room temperature for 30 minutes or for up to 1 hour.

Preheat the grill or broiler to high.

Transfer the meat directly from the marinade onto the hot grill. Reduce the heat to medium. Discard the marinade.

Grill the steaks, turning once, 6 to 8 minutes in total for medium rare. If using a broiler, leave it on high and broil the meat 6 to 8 minutes, turning once. Transfer the meat to a cutting board.

Stir the sauce ingredients together in a bowl.

Slice the steaks on the diagonal. Arrange the slices on a platter and spoon some sauce over the steaks. Serve remaining sauce on the side.

Yields 6 servings

❦ If your butcher does not have tri-tip steak, sirloin tip would do.

Grilled Marinated Veal Chops

Tender young loin veal chops can be broiled as well as grilled. In summer I serve them with a mound of greens tossed with sliced fresh peaches, toasted pecans, and red onion rings, dressed lightly with balsamic vinaigrette.

> Six 1½-inch-thick loin veal chops, trimmed of fat
> 1 tablespoon rosemary leaves, chopped fine
> 2 cloves garlic, mashed with 1½ teaspoons kosher salt
> 2 tablespoons coarsely cracked black pepper
> ¼ cup fresh lemon juice
> ½ cup olive oil

Place the veal chops in a shallow casserole just big enough to hold all of them. Mix together the rosemary, garlic paste, and pepper and rub the mixture into both sides of the chops. In a small bowl, whisk together the lemon juice and olive oil. Pour over the chops, turning once to moisten meat all around. Leave at room temperature for 30 minutes.

Preheat the grill to high. Place the chops on the grill, and if they brown too fast, lower heat to medium-high. Grill the meat 10 to 12 minutes per side, or until just cooked.

Yields 6 servings

❧ For a change, serve the chops with a lime wedge, a sauté of garden vegetables, and some crusty bread.

Grilled Lobster with Chili Butter

There is nothing better on a warm summer evening than a lobster dinner. Ask your fishmonger to cut live lobsters in half and pack them in lots of ice. Plan on grilling the lobsters within 3 hours after you get them home.

4 live lobsters, halved, 1 to 1½ pounds each

8 tablespoons (4 ounces) unsalted butter, melted

1 clove garlic, mashed with 1 teaspoon kosher salt

½ teaspoon hot chili oil

2 limes, quartered

For serving: Additional melted butter infused with more chili oil, to taste

Preheat the grill to medium-high.

Place the lobster halves, shell side down, on the hot grill.

In a small bowl, combine the butter, garlic paste, and chili oil. Brush the lobster meat with the mixture, cover the grill and cook for 12 to 14 minutes.

Place two lobster halves on each of four dinner plates. Garnish with lime wedges. Serve with additional melted butter in small bowls, one for each guest.

Yields 4 servings

Grilled Swordfish with Tomato-Pepper Sauce

Swordfish is popular both at my home and at Loaves and Fishes. I like it because it can stand up to bold seasonings like the ones below. Grilling brings out the flavor while adding a touch of smokiness. The sauce is my take on Spanish Romesco. It should be prepared about an hour before you're ready to grill the swordfish steaks.

Sauce

2 red bell peppers, quartered, seeds and inner ribs removed

2 beefsteak tomatoes, halved crosswise

1 large onion, cut into ½-inch-thick slices

¾ cup plus 2 tablespoons olive oil

1 teaspoon kosher salt

¼ cup sliced hazelnuts, toasted

1 large clove garlic, minced

3 tablespoons fresh lemon juice

½ teaspoon red pepper flakes

⅓ cup chopped fresh cilantro

Six 1¼-inch-thick swordfish steaks (2½ to 3 pounds)

¼ cup olive oil

2 teaspoons kosher salt

⅓ cup coarsely crushed black peppercorns

⅓ cup chopped fresh cilantro leaves, for garnish

2 limes cut into wedges, for garnish

To prepare the sauce, preheat the oven to 400°F. Place the peppers, tomatoes, and onions on a sheet pan. Drizzle with 2 tablespoons olive oil, sprinkle with salt, and roast 35 to 40 minutes, until the vegetables are tender. Cool slightly. Transfer to a food processor. Add the hazelnuts, garlic, lemon juice, pepper flakes, ¾ cup olive oil, and cilantro and purée until smooth. Taste for seasoning.

Preheat the grill to high.

Trim the swordfish steaks of all skin and any dark spots. Arrange the steaks on a baking sheet pan and brush thoroughly with olive oil. Sprinkle with the salt. Divide the crushed pepper evenly among the steaks, pressing it hard into both sides to make sure it adheres. Grill 3 to 4 minutes per side.

Serve garnished with cilantro and, for color, a lime wedge per plate. Nap each steak with sauce. Serve remaining sauce on the side.

Yields 6 servings

* The Tomato-Pepper Sauce makes a really fine pasta sauce. You can also make it with ½ cup of olive oil and serve it as a dip with grilled bread or raw vegetables.

* If you cannot find sliced hazelnuts, you can substitute sliced almonds.

Seared Tuna with Asian Slaw and Wasabi Cream

Tuna is at its best when it has been briefly seared on a very hot grill, keeping the center raw and juicy. Its rich flavor goes well with the tangy slaw and Wasabi Cream. Ask for "sushi-grade" tuna at your fish market; that should insure its freshness. Don't be put off by the list of ingredients—believe me, preparation goes really fast! Prepare the slaw first since it needs a little time for the seasonings to blend.

Asian Slaw

1 pound green cabbage

½ head radicchio

½ pound sugar snap peas, trimmed

1 medium carrot, peeled

1 small red onion, peeled

⅓ cup finely chopped curly parsley

1½ teaspoons kosher salt

1 teaspoon freshly ground black pepper

¼ cup safflower oil

3 tablespoons rice vinegar

1 teaspoon toasted sesame oil

1½ teaspoons sugar

Tuna

4 sushi-grade tuna steaks, 1½-inches thick (about 2 pounds), at room
    temperature

2 tablespoons olive oil

1 tablespoon coarsely ground black pepper

1 teaspoon ground coriander

1 teaspoon kosher salt

Wasabi Cream

    1 tablespoon wasabi powder

    1 tablespoon water

    ½ teaspoon rice vinegar

    1 cup mayonnaise

    ½ teaspoon kosher salt

    Fresh cilantro, for garnish

With your food processor, shred the cabbage, radicchio, snap peas, carrot, and onion. Transfer to a large bowl. Sprinkle with the parsley, salt, and pepper. Combine the safflower oil, rice vinegar, sesame oil, and sugar in a jar with a tight-fitting lid and shake well to blend. Pour the dressing over the slaw and toss well to coat all. Set aside.

Preheat the grill to high. Rub the tuna steaks with the olive oil, coarse pepper, coriander, and salt. Grill 3 to 4 minutes per side until done to your taste. Set aside on a platter.

To make the wasabi cream, stir the wasabi powder and water in a bowl to make a paste. Add the rice vinegar, mayonnaise, and salt. Whisk to combine.

To serve, place a mound of slaw on each of four dinner plates. Add the tuna steaks, garnish with the cilantro, and serve with the wasabi cream on the side.

Yields 4 servings

Scallop and Shrimp Skewers with Cilantro-Cucumber Sauce

We like serving this dish with a simple rice pilaf and a sauté of baby spinach.

1 cup fresh orange juice

½ cup fresh lime juice

2 tablespoons light brown sugar

2 cloves garlic, mashed with 1½ tablespoons kosher salt

¼ cup minced fresh cilantro

1 tablespoon seeded and minced jalapeño pepper

1½ pounds large raw shrimp, peeled and deveined (2½ pounds if bought in their shells)

18 sea scallops

9 slices bacon, cut in half crosswise

Sauce

2 cloves garlic, minced

1 cup coarsely chopped seedless cucumber, skin left on

1½ cups coarsely chopped fresh cilantro

1 cup sour cream

1¼ cups mayonnaise

½ teaspoon kosher salt

¼ teaspoon hot pepper sauce

A dozen 12-inch wooden skewers, soaked in hot water for 15 minutes prior to grilling to prevent scorching

Stir the orange and lime juice, sugar, garlic paste, cilantro, and jalapeño together in a large bowl. Add the shrimp and scallops and toss to coat. Set aside for 15 minutes to marinate at room temperature. Meanwhile, heat the grill to medium.

Grill the bacon on a baking sheet for 10 minutes until it is limp and has released most of its fat. Drain on paper towels.

Drain the scallops and shrimp and reserve the marinade. Wrap a piece of bacon around each scallop. Thread the scallops onto six skewers. Thread the shrimp onto the remaining skewers. Grill 7 to 8 minutes without turning. Transfer the skewers to a serving platter.

Cook the marinade in a small saucepan until the liquid is reduced to about ½ cup. Drizzle over the seafood skewers.

To make the sauce, place the garlic, cucumber, and cilantro in a food processor fitted with a metal blade and process until fine. Add the sour cream, mayonnaise, salt, and hot sauce. Pulse just to combine.

Offer the sauce on the side.

Yields 6 servings

⁂ If you're cooking indoors, cook the bacon in a preheated oven at 350°F for 10 to 15 minutes until the bacon is limp. Make sure not to crisp the bacon; it must remain limp so that it can be wrapped around the seafood. Broil the skewers 7 to 8 minutes.

⁂ We also use the Cilantro-Cucumber Sauce with poached chicken or as a dressing for green salads. Covered and refrigerated, it lasts for up to a week.

Citrus–Marinated Salmon

This recipe can be easily doubled.

2½ pounds skinless salmon fillet, cut into 4 equal pieces
1 cup fresh orange juice
¼ cup fresh lime juice
¼ cup fresh lemon juice
½ teaspoon kosher salt
¼ teaspoon cayenne pepper
6 tablespoons (3 ounces) unsalted butter, melted
1 tablespoon snipped chives, for garnish

Place the salmon pieces in a shallow casserole. Stir the orange, lime, and lemon juices, salt, and cayenne together in a bowl and pour over salmon. Set aside for 15 minutes at room temperature to marinate.

Preheat the grill to medium-high. Take salmon from the marinade and pat dry with paper towels. Reserve the marinade. Brush each piece of salmon generously with melted butter and place on the heated grill for 2 minutes with the lid closed. Transfer to four dinner plates, and garnish with the chives.

Pour marinade into a saucepan, set it on the grill and bring to a boil. Pour the hot marinade into a sauceboat to serve along with the salmon.

Yields 4 servings

For Those Rainy "No-Grilling" Nights

Here are a few of Loaves and Fishes' most-requested recipes that can be made either on a grill, in the oven, or on your stovetop.

Escabeche of Flounder

Escabeche is a perfect dish for a hot summer day. The marinade is intended to preserve the cooked fish; it originated in Spain, then spread throughout the Mediterranean regions. We serve this as a light lunch or as part of a dinner buffet, and it is a very popular take-out item. The fish should marinate for at least 6 hours, and up to 24 hours.

¾ cup unbleached all-purpose flour

1½ teaspoons kosher salt

1 teaspoon freshly ground black pepper

2 pounds flounder fillet

3 tablespoons olive oil

Marinade

1¼ cups red wine vinegar

½ cup cold water

¼ cup olive oil

4 cloves garlic, halved lengthwise

1 tablespoon fresh rosemary, chopped fine, plus a few sprigs for garnish

1 teaspoon sugar

½ teaspoon red pepper flakes

¼ cup currants or raisins

Combine the flour, salt, and pepper on a flat large platter. Dip the flounder into the mixture, coating both sides. Heat the olive oil in a large skillet over medium-high heat. Sauté the flounder about 5 to 7 minutes, turning once, until brown and just done. Transfer the fish to a large deep platter.

With paper towels, wipe the skillet clean. Combine the vinegar, water, oil, garlic, rosemary, sugar, pepper flakes, and currants in the skillet and bring to a boil. Lower the heat, cover, and simmer for 5 minutes. Pour the hot marinade over the flounder. Cool to room temperature. Cover and refrigerate until serving time. Garnish with rosemary sprigs.

> ※ When covered and refrigerated, the escabeche will keep for up to a week. Other fish in the flounder family such as gray or lemon sole will do just as well. Tilapia and fluke are also delicious when prepared with this tasty marinade.

Chicken Frickadellen with Caper and Lemon Topping

Translated, frickadellen *means "large meatballs, lightly flattened." We make them in large quantities at Loaves and Fishes. They're so much in demand because they are juicy and tender, and reheat well. We serve them on a toasted bun with a side of green salad, or as a dinner entrée with a side of couscous.*

2 pounds boneless chicken thighs, skinned, trimmed of fat, and cut into large chunks

1 cup minced onion

1 cup soft fresh bread crumbs

2 large eggs

2 tablespoons fresh lemon juice

1½ teaspoons kosher salt

1 teaspoon smoked Spanish paprika

1 teaspoon ground cumin

¼ teaspoon cayenne pepper

Topping

3 tablespoons olive oil

1 cup finely chopped onion

⅓ cup capers, drained

¼ cup fresh lemon juice

¼ cup minced fresh curly parsley

Place the chicken in a food processor fitted with a metal blade. Pulse a few times until coarsely chopped. Transfer into a large bowl. Add the onion, bread crumbs, eggs, lemon juice, salt, paprika, cumin, and cayenne and, using your hands, knead until well combined. Shape into 8 patties.

To grill: Brush the grill lightly with oil. Cook the patties over medium-high heat for 12 minutes, turning them once.

To sauté: Heat 2 tablespoons olive oil in a large skillet. Sauté the patties over medium heat for 12 to 14 minutes, turning them once, until cooked.

To make the topping, in the olive oil sauté the onion in a skillet over low heat for about 8 minutes until onions are light brown and glossy. Add the capers and cook 3 minutes, stirring a few times. Add the lemon juice, turn the heat to high and cook 30 seconds. Spoon the topping over the patties and sprinkle with parsley.

Yields 4 servings

This recipe can be doubled.

Oven-Fried Chicken

A James Beard–inspired recipe that we have been making for years at Loaves and Fishes.
It is really great!

Two 3-pound chickens, backs removed, each cut into 8 pieces

2 large eggs

1 tablespoon red wine vinegar

2 tablespoons kosher salt

1 teaspoon freshly ground black pepper

Crumb Coating

4 cups panko or plain dry bread crumbs

½ cup all-purpose flour

1½ teaspoons paprika

1 teaspoon dried thyme, or 2 teaspoons fresh

2 teaspoons kosher salt

1 teaspoon freshly ground black pepper

8 tablespoons (4 ounces) unsalted butter, melted

Preheat the oven to 425°F.

Place the chicken in a large bowl. Combine the eggs, vinegar, salt, and pepper in a small bowl and whisk. Pour the mixture over the chicken and toss to coat. Combine the panko, flour, paprika, thyme, salt, and pepper on a sheet pan. Dip the chicken pieces, one at a time, into the crumb mixture, coating well on all sides.

Place the chicken on one or two baking sheets, making sure to allow ample space between each piece. Pour the melted butter evenly over the chicken. Bake for 45 to 50 minutes, or until crispy brown.

To check for doneness, insert an instant-read thermometer into the thickest part of the chicken without touching the bone. It should read 165°F.

Serve hot or at room temperature.

Yields 16 pieces of chicken

Chicken Biriyani

Spices are at the heart of Indian cuisine and this chicken and rice dish is a culinary fusion of what I know and like about spices and curries. A truly tasty make-ahead one-dish meal that my family informs me is even better when it's been reheated.

½ teaspoon saffron

1 cinnamon stick

1¼ cups rice

¾ cup raisins

¼ cup peanut oil

3 cups chopped onions

1½ pounds boneless, skinless chicken breasts, cut into bite-size strips

2 teaspoons kosher salt

1 teaspoon freshly ground black pepper

1 teaspoon grated fresh ginger

2 teaspoons curry powder

1 teaspoon ground cardamom

½ teaspoon hot pepper sauce

1 cup plain yogurt

½ cup Crème Fraîche (page 30)

1 cup coarsely chopped salted cashews

½ cup chopped fresh cilantro

Pour 2½ cups water into a large heavy saucepan, add the saffron and cinnamon stick, and bring to a boil. Add the rice and simmer, covered, for 15 minutes. Add the raisins. Stir once and set aside.

In another heavy saucepan, over medium-high heat, in 2 tablespoons of the peanut oil sauté the onions. Stir often until the onions are browned. Add the onions to the rice. In the same pan, heat the remaining 2 tablespoons of peanut oil until very hot. Add the chicken pieces and sauté for 5 minutes or until chicken is just cooked and browned.

Turn heat to very low, add salt, pepper, ginger, curry powder, cardamom, hot sauce, yogurt, and crème fraîche. Stir to blend. Add chicken mixture to the rice and stir gently to combine. Remove and discard cinnamon stick. Transfer the biriyani to a serving platter. Sprinkle with cashews, garnish with cilantro, and serve.

Yields 4 servings

Apricot–Lime Baked Chicken

Bone-in chicken legs are a fabulously moist part of the chicken, which makes them ideal for reheating without drying out. We bake this ahead of time, refrigerate it, and send our customers off to the beach or picnic with a tub of chicken legs and a container of tasty apricot mayonnaise.

8 whole chicken legs, separated into thighs and drumsticks

4 cloves garlic, minced

½ cup fresh lime juice

½ cup apricot preserves

⅓ cup soy sauce

¼ cup light brown sugar

½ teaspoon hot pepper sauce

1 box peppery daikon sprouts, trimmed

Apricot Mayonnaise

1½ cups mayonnaise

⅓ cup apricot preserves

1 tablespoon curry powder

2 teaspoons fresh lemon juice

½ teaspoon kosher salt

Preheat the oven to 425°F.

Arrange the chicken legs in a single layer, skin down, in a large roasting pan. Place the garlic, lime juice, apricot preserves, soy sauce, sugar, and hot sauce in a food processor fitted with a metal blade, and purée until smooth. Pour the mixture over the chicken and bake 1¼ hours, turning the chicken once after 40 minutes.

Sprinkle daikon sprouts over a serving platter and pile the cooked chicken on top.

To make the apricot mayonnaise, place the mayonnaise, apricot preserves, curry powder, lemon juice, and salt in a bowl. Stir to blend well. Transfer to a serving bowl to offer alongside the chicken.

Yields 8 servings

❈ If you cannot find peppery daikon sprouts, substitute radish sprouts, which have a similar peppery taste.

Coconut Shrimp

A lovely platter piled with these golden brown, crispy delights always evokes smiles. Everyone automatically gravitates to the spot where the platter is placed and lingers there, chatting, until every last shrimp is gone.

1 pound (24 count) shrimp, peeled and deveined

2 teaspoons grated lime zest

1 tablespoon fresh lime juice

1 cup unbleached all-purpose flour

1 teaspoon kosher salt

1 teaspoon freshly ground black pepper

2 large eggs

½ cup unsweetened coconut milk

2½ cups sweetened flaked coconut

1 teaspoon curry powder

3 cups peanut oil, for frying

Combine the shrimp, lime zest, and juice, and set aside. Mix the flour, salt, and pepper in a shallow bowl and set aside. Beat the eggs and coconut milk in a shallow bowl until smooth. Mix the coconut flakes and curry powder together and spread the mixture on a flat plate.

Coat one shrimp at a time, first with flour, then egg, then coconut. Place each coated shrimp on a sheet pan. Repeat until all shrimp are coated.

Pour the peanut oil into a heavy skillet and heat to 375°F over high heat. Drop the shrimp into the hot oil, 6 at a time. Fry about 2 to 3 minutes, turning once, until golden brown. Drain on paper towels. Repeat until all shrimp are fried. Serve hot.

❆ The shrimp can be prepared 2 hours ahead of time and reheated in a 375°F oven for 10 minutes.

❆ Needless to say, this can be served as one of the best, most popular starters ever. The coconut shrimp go so quickly that you might have to double the recipe to satisfy your guests!

Shrimp Cakes with Herb Mayonnaise

These should be called seafood cakes, since you could substitute lobster meat, crabmeat, or scallops and turn out delicious variations of these crispy, oh-so-good, shrimp cakes. This is another recipe that can be prepared on the grill or stovetop.

2 tablespoons olive oil

1 cup finely chopped shallots (3 large)

¾ cup finely chopped celery

2 pounds small shrimp, peeled and deveined

¼ cup finely chopped curly parsley

¼ cup finely chopped fresh dill

1 teaspoon kosher salt

¼ teaspoon cayenne pepper

1 cup mayonnaise

1½ cups dry bread crumbs

1 cup sliced almonds

6 tablespoons clarified butter, for frying

Herb Mayonnaise

¼ cup chopped fresh chives

¼ cup chopped fresh dill

¼ cup chopped curly parsley

3 tablespoons milk

1 tablespoon fresh lime juice

½ teaspoon salt

½ teaspoon sugar

¼ teaspoon hot pepper sauce

1¼ cups mayonnaise

In a skillet over medium heat, warm the olive oil. Sauté the shallots and celery until the vegetables appear glossy. Set aside to cool.

Place the shrimp in a food processor fitted with a metal blade. Pulse three times to chop shrimp a bit. Transfer to a large bowl. Add the parsley, dill, salt, cayenne, mayonnaise, and ½ cup of the bread crumbs.

In a separate deep, wide bowl, combine the remaining cup of bread crumbs with the almonds. Set it aside.

Knead the shrimp mixture to thoroughly blend all the ingredients. With your hands, shape into 12 balls. Roll each ball in the bread crumb–almond mixture. Coat completely. With your palms, flatten the balls into disks.

Using a grill or stovetop at high heat, sauté the shrimp cakes with clarified butter in a large skillet for 10 to 12 minutes total, until the cakes are crispy and just cooked.

To make the herb mayonnaise: purée the chives, dill, parsley, milk, and lime juice until smooth. Fold in the salt, sugar, hot sauce, and mayonnaise. Stir well and serve with the shrimp cakes.

Yields 6 to 8 servings

Pan-Fried Striped Bass with Tomato-Butter Sauce

In our local fish markets on the tip of Long Island we have striped bass available to us from July 1 to December 1. At Loaves and Fishes, we have used cod and halibut as alternatives to the bass and found it equally wonderful. Pan-frying the fish with a panko crumb coating creates a really nice, crunchy crust.

½ cup Crème Fraîche (page 30)

2 tablespoons Dijon mustard

1 cup panko or other dry bread crumbs

2 teaspoons kosher salt

2 teaspoons freshly ground black pepper

Four 6-ounce striped bass fillets, of equal thickness

2 tablespoons safflower oil

2 tablespoons (1 ounce) unsalted butter

Sauce

12 tablespoons (6 ounces) cold unsalted butter, in 1-tablespoon slices

¼ cup finely chopped shallots

1 cup peeled, seeded, finely chopped tomatoes

2 tablespoons sherry vinegar

½ cup dry white wine

½ teaspoon kosher salt

½ teaspoon freshly ground black pepper

1 tablespoon chopped fresh chives

Combine the Crème Fraîche and mustard in a small bowl and stir to blend. Combine the panko, salt, and pepper on a large flat plate. Coat the fish on both sides with the Crème Fraîche. Dip it next into the panko, pressing down on the fish to make the crumbs adhere.

Heat the safflower oil and butter in a large skillet until hot. Place fish in the skillet, cover and cook over a medium-high heat for 2 minutes. Using 2 spatulas, carefully turn the fish over and cook for an additional 2 to 3 minutes. Do not overcook. Transfer the fish onto four warm dinner plates. Wipe the skillet clean with paper towels.

To make the sauce, heat 2 tablespoons of butter in the skillet. Add the shallots and sauté for 2 minutes over medium heat. Stir in the tomatoes, vinegar, and wine. Cook 2 more minutes. Add the salt and pepper. Reduce the heat to low. Using a wire whisk, swirl and blend in the remaining butter, adding 1 tablespoon at a time. Whisk until the sauce thickens slightly. Do not allow the sauce to come to a boil after the butter has been added. Distribute the sauce evenly around the fish. Sprinkle with chives and serve.

Yields 4 servings

Wiener Schnitzel with Brown Butter and Capers

In the late summer of 1986, I spent seven weeks at the American Embassy in Vienna cooking all sorts of Austrian dishes. This recipe stands out as one of the all-time favorites and is surprisingly easy to prepare.

Kosher salt

4 slices top-quality veal cut from center rump, 4 ounces each, ⅛-inch thick

½ cup unbleached all-purpose flour

2 large eggs beaten

2 tablespoons water

2 cups dry bread crumbs

1 teaspoon freshly ground black pepper

¼ cup olive oil

6 tablespoons (3 ounces) unsalted butter

¼ cup capers, drained

8 lemon wedges

Lightly salt the slices of veal. Place the flour in a shallow bowl. Beat the eggs and water in another. Mix the bread crumbs, 2 teaspoons salt, and the pepper in a third bowl. Dip each veal slice first into the flour and shake off any excess, then coat each with the egg mixture, and finally dip the slices into the bread crumbs. With your hands, press the bread crumbs into each veal slice so each is completely covered. Shake off excess.

Heat olive oil with 2 tablespoons of the butter in a large skillet. When the butter is very hot, sauté the veal slices 2 to 3 minutes per side. Transfer the veal onto warmed dinner plates.

Add the remaining butter and the capers to the skillet and fry 2 minutes over high heat, stirring a few times. Sprinkle capers over the crispy veal and serve with wedges of lemon.

Yields 4 servings

Baked Flounder and Shrimp in Wine-Dill Sauce

This was my mother's answer to a speedy dinner. Flounder, sole, and fluke, plentiful in the Baltic Sea, were available to us fresh every day. I make this often when pressed for time.

2 tablespoons butter

⅓ cup finely chopped shallots

1 small tomato, chopped fine

8 flounder fillets

12 large shrimp, peeled and deveined

Kosher salt and freshly ground black pepper to taste

½ cup dry white wine

¾ cup heavy cream

1 tablespoon chopped fresh dill

Preheat the oven to 400°F. Butter an ovenproof stainless-steel skillet. Sprinkle the shallots and tomato evenly over bottom of pan. Season flounder with salt and pepper. Fold each fillet in half and place in one layer around the inside perimeter of pan. Arrange shrimp in the center. Season with salt and pepper. Pour wine and cream over fish and bring to a boil on stovetop. Cover the pan with parchment paper or foil and bake 12 minutes. Sprinkle with dill and serve.

Yields 4 servings

> ❧ We always had small boiled potatoes and cucumber or green salad served with this fish dish. I like it served simply with French bread and any kind of leafy green salad, too.

Halibut Baked with Olives, Lemon, and Fresh Basil

I relish all kinds of warm weather foods, but this one, I think, is exceptional for its taste, texture, and the ease in which it can be prepared. Mind you, any lean white fish will do. I serve this with cooked rice since it blends in so beautifully with the sauce and absorbs its taste.

½ cup olive oil

2 pounds halibut fillet, 1½-inches thick, cut into 4 pieces

1 small red onion, cut into paper-thin slices

3 cloves garlic, sliced as thin as possible

1 large ripe tomato, sliced thin

1 lemon, sliced very thin and pitted

⅓ cup pitted Niçoise olives

1 teaspoon kosher salt

1 teaspoon freshly ground black pepper

½ cup chopped fresh basil leaves

1 teaspoon fresh thyme leaves or ½ teaspoon dried

Preheat the oven to 400°F.

Brush 2 tablespoons of the olive oil over the bottom of a 13 x 9-inch glass baking dish. Place the fish in the dish, spacing the pieces evenly. Scatter the onion, garlic, tomato, lemon slices, and olives uniformly over the fish. Sprinkle with salt, pepper, ¼ cup of the basil, and the thyme. Pour the remaining olive oil over all, so that fish and vegetables are thinly coated. Place the dish in the oven and bake 25 minutes without opening the oven door.

Garnish with the remaining basil and serve.

Yields 4 servings

✳ This recipe can be expanded to serve 6 by simply using 1½ times these ingredients.

✳ f you have a pretty casserole of the same dimensions that is ovenproof, use it. In that way, it can easily go from oven to table.

Bouillabaisse

My dear friend Ina Garten makes the best version of this simple seafood stew that I have ever tasted. I was thrilled when she offered me this recipe from Barefoot in Paris, *her wonderfully inspiring book. Use whatever seafood is best and freshest at your seafood shop.*

3 tablespoons olive oil

2 cups finely chopped onion

2 cups peeled and chopped potatoes

2 cups finely chopped fennel (1 large bulb)

2 teaspoons kosher salt

1 teaspoon freshly ground black pepper

½ teaspoon red pepper flakes

2 cups dry white wine

1 quart fish stock or bottled clam juice

One 28-ounce can chopped plum tomatoes

3 cloves garlic, minced

1 teaspoon saffron

1 pound peeled and deveined shrimp (24 count)

2 pounds firm lean white fish such as halibut, cod, or monkfish, cut into
  large chunks

3 pounds littleneck clams, scrubbed

Two 5-inch strips orange zest

1 tablespoon minced curly parsley, for garnish

Place the olive oil, onion, potatoes, fennel, salt, pepper, and pepper flakes in a large heavy soup pot. Sauté over medium heat for 10 minutes or until onions look glossy.

Add the wine, fish stock, tomatoes with their juice, garlic, and saffron. Cover and bring to a boil. Lower the heat and simmer, covered, for 20 minutes.

Add the shrimp, fish chunks, clams, and orange zest. Bring to a boil and cook, covered, for 5 minutes or until fish is cooked through and clams have opened. Remove from the heat. Discard the orange zest.

Serve hot, garnished with minced parsley.

Yields 6 servings

Desserts

Now we come to the grand finale, the irresistible and luxurious part of the meal. My favorite, too.

I truly believe that if you serve a fabulous, knockout dessert, chances are your guests may not remember what they had for dinner. Dessert always brings smiles to the table and no matter how full people claim they are, there always seems to be just a little bit of special space left over for dessert. The last taste savored, the punctuation to the meal, is the one that seems to linger the longest.

I am not a chocoholic, but some of my best friends are and so is our son Harm who, for many years, served as my guinea pig when it came to testing and tasting new chocolate concoctions that I had dreamed up. There we would sit, the kitchen still bathed in its wonderful chocolaty fragrance, Harm and I across from each other; he tasting, mmmmm-ing, moaning, wearing such a blissfully happy smile; I tasting, noting any remarks he may have had. It was such a bonding time for us. It was heaven!

Sweets are an essential part of the day. It's what many of us yearn for around four in the afternoon—tea-time, a time when we sorely need an energy pick-me-up! I always reach for a cup of strong coffee and a cookie. Sometimes a slice of layer cake will hit the spot, or a simple muffin, anything that satisfies that craving and will send us off recharged and rolling up our sleeves ready to attack the rest of the day with a bit more vigor and enthusiasm.

This section of the book has been designed to make use of as many of the abundant and magnificent gifts provided to us by Mother Nature as we can. Summer fruits are divine: raw, sprinkled with sugar, dolloped with whipped cream, crème fraîche, or ice cream; and made into ice cream, sorbets, jams, preserves, pies, crumbles, cakes, cookies, muffins. The selection and the options are infinite.

When I was a child, every summer we would pick bushels of fresh fruits from our gardens and orchard, leaving my mother to become as creative as she could, impelled by her determination to not waste a thing. Those fruits that weren't enjoyed fresh and didn't go into baking were made into soups, sauces, and jams. Since we didn't have a freezer, surplus had to be preserved and then stored in our basement. My sisters and I would join our mother in the kitchen, with mountains of fruits in the center of our table, tubs of sugar to the side, a large pot of boiling water on the stove, and on the sideboard a line of pristine glass jars with their lids. Thus began our yearly chore of preserving fruits that we would then carefully transport to the cool, dark basement where they would neatly line the shelves my father had built for this specific purpose.

In the middle of winter, with a relentless chill gripping at our fingers and toes, the winds whistling through invisible cracks in the farmhouse, the sun hiding for most of the day, I would love to take the lid off of a jar of preserved peaches or plums, and have my senses suddenly reignited as a whiff of summer floated out to remind me of what we were missing and what we had to look forward to. It would set me counting the days to that magical time when I would spy the first green sprout nosing its way out of the thawing earth next to our back door, and a tiny, tight bud stretching out to find the first rays of sun.

Summer! Ah!

Strawberry Pie

When strawberry season begins, I'm among the first ones lining up outside our local farm stands. Detlef and I, with our grandchildren in tow, used to pick strawberries ourselves. They ate more than they collected, but that was part of the fun. We buy tons of freshly picked strawberries, still warm from the sun; they send out the most tantalizing aromas that linger for hours. I try to incorporate them into as many recipes as I can think up. Here's a very popular one.

Crust

1½ cups graham cracker crumbs

⅔ cup sugar

1 teaspoon ground cinnamon

½ teaspoon freshly ground black pepper

6 tablespoons (3 ounces) unsalted butter, melted

Filling

8 cups strawberries, rinsed and hulled

⅓ cup water

1¼ cups sugar

⅓ cup cornstarch

Grated zest of 1 orange

1 teaspoon ground cinnamon

1 tablespoon framboise, optional

Whipped cream or vanilla ice cream, for serving

Preheat the oven to 375°F. Butter a 9 x 2-inch pie dish. Combine the crumbs, sugar, cinnamon, pepper, and butter in a large bowl and mix well. Press the mixture into the buttered pie dish and bake for 12 to 15 minutes, or until the crust turns light brown. Set it aside to cool.

Place 5 cups of the strawberries in a large saucepan and mash, using a potato masher, until totally crushed. Add the water, sugar, cornstarch, orange zest, and cinnamon. Bring the mixture to a boil over medium-high heat. Continue to cook, stirring constantly, until the mixture turns thick and glossy. Remove the pan from the stove and fold in remaining strawberries and the framboise, if using. Pour the filling into the pie shell and spread evenly over the bottom. Chill the pie 4 to 6 hours, or more. Serve with whipped cream or ice cream.

Yields 6 to 8 servings

Blueberry Crumble

If the notion of making a pie seems like too much work, try this homey dessert. It never fails to please guests. This too can be served warm with a scoop of ice cream on top.

Filling

7 cups fresh blueberries, rinsed and picked over

1¼ cups sugar

¼ cup cornstarch

¼ cup fresh lemon juice

1 teaspoon ground cinnamon

Crumble

½ cup unbleached all-purpose flour

½ cup rolled oats

½ cup chopped walnuts

½ teaspoon ground cinnamon

6 tablespoons (3 ounces) unsalted butter, cut into pieces

Preheat the oven to 400°F. Butter a 2-quart casserole.

Combine the blueberries, sugar, cornstarch, lemon juice, and cinnamon in a large bowl and blend well. Pour the blueberry mixture into the casserole and cover loosely with foil. Bake for 15 minutes. Lower oven temperature to 375°F and bake for 20 minutes longer.

Combine the flour, oats, walnuts, cinnamon, and butter in a large bowl. Mix it with your hands until the texture becomes crumbly.

Take the casserole from the oven. Discard the foil. Sprinkle the crumble evenly over the hot blueberries. Return the casserole to the oven. Bake 30 minutes more, or until the topping is brown and the blueberry filling is bubbling. Cool 2 hours or more before serving.

Yields 6 to 8 servings

Rhubarb–Blueberry Pie

There are two types of blueberries that appear on farm stands and markets in June and July. The small ones are wild, the larger ones are cultivated. We use the larger ones in this pie where their natural sweetness complements the tartness of the rhubarb. This pie can be made early in the day and left at room temperature until serving time, then watch it disappear.

Crust

2 cups unbleached all-purpose flour

¼ teaspoon kosher salt

2 tablespoons sugar

16 tablespoons (8 ounces) cold unsalted butter, cut into small cubes

2 teaspoons fresh lemon juice

6 to 7 tablespoons ice water

Filling

3 cups fresh blueberries, rinsed and picked over

4 cups ½-inch-sliced rhubarb

1¼ cups sugar

Grated zest of 1 small orange

½ teaspoon ground cinnamon

¼ cup cornstarch

1 egg yolk

1 tablespoon heavy cream

¼ cup coarse sugar

Place the flour, salt, and sugar in a food processor fitted with a metal blade and process to blend. Add the butter and pulse 5 times. Add the juice. With the motor running, pour in 6 to 7 tablespoons water through the feed tube and process until the dough clings together in clumps. Gather the pastry into a ball, cover, and chill for 30 minutes.

Preheat the oven to 350°F.

Place the blueberries, rhubarb, sugar, orange zest, cinnamon, and cornstarch in a large bowl, toss well to blend. Set aside.

Cut the dough in half. On a lightly floured surface, roll out one half into a 12-inch round. Transfer the round to a 9-inch pie dish. Spoon in the filling, spreading it evenly over the bottom.

Roll out second half to an 11-inch round. Place over the filling. Seal and crimp the edges.

Whisk the yolk and cream together and brush it on the pie top and over the edges. Sprinkle with the coarse sugar, bake 50 minutes to 1 hour. Cool to room temperature.

Serves 6 to 8

Rhubarb Muffins with Coconut Topping

Around three or four in the afternoon, we have customers coming to our store looking for something a little sweet to have with coffee or tea. This muffin is often their choice.

Crumb Topping

½ cup unbleached all-purpose flour

1 cup sweetened shredded coconut

1 cup sugar

1 cup coarsely chopped walnuts

8 tablespoons (4 ounces) cold unsalted butter, cut into small cubes

3 cups unbleached all-purpose flour

1¼ cups sugar

¼ teaspoon kosher salt

1 tablespoon baking powder

2 large eggs

16 tablespoons (8 ounces) unsalted butter, melted and cooled

½ cup milk

½ cup heavy cream

Grated zest of 2 oranges

3 cups thinly sliced rhubarb

To make the topping, place the flour, coconut, sugar, walnuts, and butter in a bowl. Mix with your hands until crumbly. Set it aside.

Preheat the oven to 375°F and line a 12-cup muffin pan with paper liners.

Combine the flour, sugar, salt, and baking powder in a large bowl. Add the eggs, melted butter, milk, cream, and orange zest. Stir just to blend well. Fold in the rhubarb. Spoon the batter into the paper-lined muffin pan. Divide the topping over the muffins, and bake for 25 to 30 minutes. Insert a wooden tooth-pick into the center of a muffin. If it comes out clean, the muffin is done.

Yields 12

❧ The crumb topping can also be used instead of a top crust on any fruit pie.

Peach Tart with Almond Topping and a Cookie Crust

Ripe peaches fresh from the fruit stand are best when simply peeled, sliced, and eaten as is. This tart is a close second. Serve with ice cream or whipped cream.

Crust

1¼ cups unbleached all-purpose flour

1 tablespoon sugar

8 tablespoons (4 ounces) cold unsalted butter, cut into small pieces

1 egg yolk

¼ cup very cold water

2 tablespoons (1 ounce) unsalted butter, melted

Filling

⅓ cup apricot preserves

7 peaches (about 2 pounds), peeled, pitted, and sliced

4 tablespoons (2 ounces) unsalted butter, softened

¼ cup sliced almonds

⅓ cup sugar

2 tablespoons cornstarch

To make the crust, place the flour, sugar, and butter in a food processor fitted with the steel blade. Pulse the mixture 4 times. Add the egg yolk and, with the motor running, pour the water into the feed tube. Process until dough starts to cling together.

Transfer the dough to a countertop and gather it into a ball. Cover and refrigerate the dough for 30 minutes or longer.

Brush the melted butter onto the bottom and sides of a 9-inch tart pan with a removable bottom.

Roll out the chilled dough on a lightly floured surface to ¼-inch thickness. Fit into tart pan, pressing dough over the bottom and up the sides. Freeze the tart shell 30 minutes. Meanwhile, preheat the oven to 400°F.

From freezer to oven, bake the shell 15 minutes.

Spread the apricot preserves with a brush over the bottom of the baked crust. Arrange the peaches evenly over the preserves. Dot with the softened butter. Scatter the almonds over the top. Mix the sugar and cornstarch together and sprinkle it over the tart. Bake 45 minutes. Cool.

Yields 6 to 8 servings

Two Plum Tarts

What is summer without a tart made from the ripest, juiciest, sweetest plums? These tarts disappear moments after they're put on our Loaves and Fishes shelves. That's why I thought it best to double this recipe.

4 cups unbleached all-purpose flour

1½ cups finely chopped walnuts

1½ packed cups light brown sugar

24 tablespoons (12 ounces) cold unsalted butter, cut into 1-tablespoon slices

2 egg yolks

4 pounds ripe Italian prune plums, pitted and quartered lengthwise

Preheat the oven to 400°F.

Combine the flour, walnuts, and sugar in a large bowl. Add the butter and the egg yolks and mix by hand or with an electric mixer until crumbly.

Press 3 cups of the crumb mixture into each of two 9- or 10-inch spring-form pans, creating an even layer over the bottom of each pan. Beginning from the outer edge of each pan, arrange the plums in a circular, flowerlike pattern, skin side down, over the doughy layer. Sprinkle the remaining crumb mixture uniformly over the plums.

Bake 50 to 55 minutes, or until lightly browned and the plum juice has risen to the top. Remove from oven and cool 10 minutes. Transfer the tarts from the pans to flat cake plates. Serve warm or at room temperature.

Yields 2 tarts, 8 to 10 servings each

Apricot Kuchen

This should be made when apricots, peaches, and other stone fruits are at their peak. On hot days, I do all my baking in the morning when the kitchen is cool. The end results are unquestionably worth the effort. It makes a wonderful afternoon treat.

8 tablespoons (4 ounces) unsalted butter, softened

1 cup sugar

1 teaspoon vanilla extract

1 tablespoon Cognac

1 large egg

1 cup unbleached all-purpose flour

1 teaspoon baking powder

½ cup sour cream

10 ripe apricots, halved and pitted

Preheat the oven to 350°F. Butter a 9-inch springform pan.

Beat the butter, ¾ cup of the sugar, the vanilla, and Cognac in an electric stand mixer until light and fluffy. Add the egg. Mix to blend. In a separate bowl, combine the flour and baking powder. Add half to the creamed mixture. Mix to blend. Add half the sour cream. Mix to blend. Add the remaining flour and sour cream. Beat well, scraping down the sides, until the batter is fully combined.

Transfer the batter to the springform pan and smooth the top. Arrange the apricots, skin side down, overlapping slightly to cover the top of the batter. Sprinkle with the remaining ¼ cup sugar. Bake 40 to 50 minutes, or until a tester inserted into the center comes out clean. Cool and serve at room temperature.

❈ This is really wonderful topped with quartered plums or peaches and nectarines cut into eighths.

Lemon Torte with Berries and Cream

Lemon, berries, and cream: the essence of summer.

7 large eggs, separated

1¼ cups sugar

⅓ cup fresh lemon juice

½ cup cornstarch

½ teaspoon baking powder

1 tablespoon unsalted butter, softened

Topping

1 cup heavy cream

2 tablespoons confectioners' sugar

1 cup each of fresh strawberries, raspberries, and blueberries, rinsed and
dried

Preheat the oven to 350°F.

Place the egg yolks and 1 cup of the sugar into the bowl of an electric stand mixer fitted with a whisk attachment. Whisk at high speed until the mixture is light and can form a thick ribbon. Add the lemon juice, cornstarch, and baking powder, and mix to combine.

In a clean bowl, with a clean whisk, beat the egg whites until foamy. Keep beating, while gradually adding the remaining sugar until the egg whites stiffen. Be careful not to overbeat.

Using a rubber spatula, gently fold the egg whites into the egg yolk mixture until just combined.

Butter only the bottom of a 9-inch springform pan with the softened butter.

Pour the batter into the pan and bake 35 to 40 minutes. Cool to room temperature.

Whip the cream with the confectioners' sugar to firm peaks. Ease the torte onto a cake platter and generously slather it with the whipped cream. Top it with the fresh berries.

Yields 8 to 10 servings

Coconut-Lemon Layer Cake

The basic cake recipe below is Loaves and Fishes' all-purpose cake that lends itself to many variations. To make our signature coconut cake we fill it with homemade lemon curd, cover the cake with a creamy icing, and coat it all over with a snowy white coconut topping. No matter how many we can supply on a daily basis, there is never one left at the end of the day.

1¾ cups unbleached all-purpose flour

¼ cup cornstarch

1 teaspoon baking powder

½ teaspoon baking soda

20 tablespoons (10 ounces) unsalted butter, softened

1¼ cups sugar

3 large eggs, separated

1 teaspoon vanilla extract

⅔ cup milk

Preheat the oven to 350°F. Butter a 9-inch springform pan. Set aside.

Sift the flour, cornstarch, baking powder, and baking soda into a large bowl. Using an electric stand mixer, beat the butter with 1 cup of sugar for about 5 minutes at high speed, until light in color. Add the egg yolks and vanilla and beat to blend. Alternately, beat in the milk and flour mixture, ending with the flour. Scrape the batter into the bowl that held the flour.

Wash and dry the mixer bowl thoroughly, then pour in the egg whites. Using the whisk attachment, beat at high speed until foamy. With the motor running, gradually whisk in the remaining sugar until soft peaks hold. Transfer the egg whites to the top of the batter and, with a rubber spatula, gently fold the egg whites into the batter. Scrape the batter into the springform pan. Smooth out the top.

Bake 45 to 50 minutes, until a toothpick inserted into the center comes out clean. Cool on a rack for 1 hour. Undo the springform pan and, using a metal spatula, slide the cake onto a plate. Wrap well with plastic wrap.

Lemon Curd

6 large egg yolks
1¼ cups sugar
½ cup fresh lemon juice
16 tablespoons (8 ounces) cold unsalted butter, cut into small pieces
Grated zest of 3 lemons

In a large heavy saucepan, whisk together the egg yolks and sugar until creamy. Add the lemon juice and butter. Cook over medium heat, stirring constantly, until it starts to bubble and has thickened. Stir in the lemon zest. Chill until very cold and thick or overnight.

Icing

2½ cups heavy cream, chilled
¾ cup confectioners' sugar
1 cup sour cream, chilled

1½ cups sweetened shredded coconut

Whisk the cream and sugar together until it holds firm peaks. With a rubber spatula, fold in the sour cream.

To assemble: cut the cake horizontally into 3 layers. Spread half the lemon curd over the bottom layer. Top with the second layer and spread with the remaining lemon curd. Top with the final layer. Spread the icing over the top and the sides of the cake. Press the coconut all over the outside of the cake.

Yields 12 servings

❊ The cake can be assembled up to 2 days ahead of time. Store the cake in the refrigerator, loosely covered, and bring it to room temperature before serving.

To make a Strawberry Layer Cake

½ cup strawberry preserves

2 pints fresh strawberries, rinsed, hulled, 8 reserved for garnish and the rest thinly sliced

4 cups heavy cream, sweetened with ½ cup superfine sugar

Spread the strawberry preserves across the bottom layer of the cake. Arrange strawberries over the preserves, then spread whipped cream onto the layer. Repeat with the middle layer. Top with the third layer. Slather the cake all over with more whipped cream and garnish with whole strawberries.

To make Peaches and Cream Cake

Use peach preserves and 6 peeled fresh, ripe peaches instead of the strawberries.

Chocolate Chunk—Orange Cake

16 tablespoons (8 ounces) unsalted butter, softened

2½ cups sugar

6 large eggs

1 tablespoon grated orange zest

3 cups unbleached all-purpose flour

1 teaspoon baking powder

1 cup sour cream

8 ounces semisweet chocolate, cut into chunks

Glaze

1 cup fresh orange juice

¼ cup fresh lemon juice

¾ cup sugar

Preheat the oven to 350°F. Butter a 10-inch Bundt or tube pan.

With an electric mixer, cream the butter and sugar until light and fluffy. Blend in the eggs, two at a time. Add the orange zest, 2 cups of the flour, baking powder, and sour cream. Beat to combine. Add the remaining flour and chocolate chunks. Beat at low speed until no traces of flour remain. Spoon the batter into the pan.

Bake for 1 hour and 15 minutes or until a toothpick inserted into the center comes out clean. Cool 5 minutes in the pan.

In a small saucepan, combine the orange juice, lemon juice, and sugar and heat until the sugar has dissolved. Drizzle over the cake. Let stand 15 minutes before unmolding the cake onto a serving plate. Cool completely before serving.

Yields 30 thin slices

❊ Tightly wrapped, the cake will keep up to a week in the refrigerator.

Banana Birthday Cake

We whip up this scrumptious cake throughout the year for just about any occasion under the sun. It's that easy and that delicious!

16 tablespoons (8 ounces) unsalted butter, softened

2 cups sugar

2 teaspoons vanilla extract

2 large eggs

4 bananas, peeled and fork-mashed

2 cups unbleached all-purpose flour

⅔ cup cornstarch

½ teaspoon kosher salt

1 teaspoon baking soda

1 teaspoon baking powder

⅔ cup milk

1 cup finely chopped walnuts

Frosting

8 ounces cream cheese, softened

4 tablespoons (2 ounces) unsalted butter, softened

4 cups confectioners' sugar

½ teaspoon vanilla extract

1 tablespoon grated orange zest

Preheat the oven to 350°F. Butter a 10-inch springform pan.

Using an electric mixer, cream the butter and sugar for 5 minutes, until light. Add the vanilla, eggs, and bananas. Beat at medium speed until well blended. Add the flour, cornstarch, salt, baking soda, baking powder, milk, and walnuts and mix at low speed for 3 minutes, until well combined.

Pour the batter into the pan. Smooth the top. Bake 1¼ hours, or until a toothpick inserted into the cake's center comes out clean. Remove from oven and let the cake cool in the pan.

To make the frosting, beat together the cream cheese, butter, sugar, vanilla, and orange zest with an electric mixer for about 7 minutes, until smooth.

Unmold the cooled cake onto a flat plate. Cut it in half horizontally. Spread 1 cup of the frosting over the bottom layer. Cover with the top layer. Slather the top and sides with the remaining frosting. Store, covered, at room temperature until ready to serve.

Yields 12 servings

Chocolate Chocolate Cake

Irresistible and one of my very own all-time favorites.

16 tablespoons (8 ounces) unsalted butter, softened

2¾ cups sugar

2½ cups unbleached all-purpose flour

1 teaspoon baking soda

¾ cup sifted cocoa (I use Droste)

1 teaspoon ground cinnamon

1 cup brewed coffee

2 teaspoons vanilla extract

1 cup sour cream

5 egg whites

Frosting

4 tablespoons (2 ounces) unsalted butter, softened

1 pound confectioners' sugar

¾ cup cocoa, sifted (Droste)

½ cup water

Preheat the oven to 325°F. Butter two 9-inch springform pans.

Using an electric mixer, cream together the butter and sugar until light. Add 1 cup of the flour, the baking soda, cocoa, cinnamon, coffee, and vanilla. Beat at low speed for about 5 minutes, until fluffy. Add the remaining flour and the sour cream. Beat at low speed until ingredients are well blended.

In a separate bowl, beat the egg whites until they hold soft peaks. With a rubber spatula, gently fold the egg whites into the chocolate batter until no white streaks show. Pour the batter into the buttered pans and spread evenly.

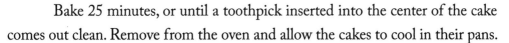

Bake 25 minutes, or until a toothpick inserted into the center of the cake comes out clean. Remove from the oven and allow the cakes to cool in their pans.

To make the frosting, beat the butter, confectioners' sugar, cocoa, and water until light and spreadable.

Unmold one of the cakes onto a cake plate. Spread frosting over the top. Top with the other layer. Slather the remaining frosting on the top and sides of the cake. Cover and store at room temperature.

Yields 10 to 12 servings

※ Kept at room temperature, and covered or wrapped tightly, this cake can last up to 5 days.

Individual Chocolate–Strawberry Trifles with Raspberry Sauce

Don't be put off by the list of ingredients. This is really very easy to prepare and can become your star dessert.

6 large eggs, at room temperature

¾ cup sugar

1 teaspoon vanilla extract

⅔ cup flour

⅓ cup cocoa

½ teaspoon freshly ground black pepper

1 teaspoon baking powder

4 tablespoons (2 ounces) unsalted butter, melted and cooled

3 cups strawberries, rinsed, hulled, and halved

¾ cup sugar

4 cups fresh raspberries, rinsed and dried

⅓ cup water

1 tablespoon framboise

Topping

2 cups heavy cream

3 tablespoons superfine sugar

1 teaspoon vanilla extract

½ cup sour cream

Preheat the oven to 350°F. Butter a 13 x 9 x 2-inch baking pan.

Place the eggs, sugar, and vanilla in the bowl of an electric mixer fitted with a whisk attachment. Beat for 5 minutes at high speed until the mixture has tripled in volume and forms thick ribbons when the whisk is lifted.

Sift the flour, cocoa, pepper, and baking powder over the egg mixture and, using a rubber spatula, fold in the dry ingredients until just blended. Fold in the melted butter gently, so as not to deflate the batter. Pour the batter into the prepared pan.

Bake 25 minutes. Let the cake cool in the pan.

Combine the strawberries and ¼ cup of the sugar in a bowl and set it aside to marinate at room temperature for 30 minutes.

To make the raspberry sauce, place the raspberries, the remaining ½ cup sugar, the water, and framboise in a food processor and purée until smooth. Set it aside until you are ready to serve.

Using an electric mixer, whisk together the heavy cream, sugar, and vanilla until firm peaks hold. Fold in the sour cream by hand.

Unmold the cake and cut into 12 pieces. Place one piece on each of six dessert plates.

Distribute half the whipped cream over the top of the cakes. Spoon half the strawberries over the cream. Cover each with the remaining portions of cake and spoon the remaining cream and strawberries over each. Drizzle the Raspberry Sauce around (not on) the stacked cakes.

Yields 6 servings

* The cake can be made the day before and stored, covered, at room temperature.

* The Raspberry Sauce can also be made a day ahead and stored, covered in the refrigerator.

Baked Chocolate Pudding with Chantilly Cream and Fresh Berries

This dessert is wonderfully rich and gooey. It will definitely please anyone passionate about chocolate. Easy to prepare, it can be made up to three days before serving. Cover, refrigerate, and bring to room temperature before serving. Serve with Chantilly cream and the sweetest, ripest, seasonal berries you can find.

4 large eggs

2 cups sugar

Seeds of 1 vanilla bean

1 tablespoon framboise (optional)

¾ cup cocoa, sifted

½ cup unbleached all-purpose flour, sifted

16 tablespoons (8 ounces) unsalted butter, melted and slightly cooled

Chantilly Cream

1 cup heavy cream

1 tablespoon superfine sugar

1 teaspoon vanilla extract

1 pint seasonal berries, rinsed, dried, and sliced, if using strawberries

Preheat the oven to 325°F. Lightly butter a shallow 2-quart casserole.

Beat the eggs and sugar with an electric mixer until light and fluffy, and the mixture has quadrupled in volume. Add the vanilla bean seeds, framboise (if using), the cocoa, and flour. Mix at low speed until combined. Add the butter and mix to blend. Transfer batter to the casserole.

Place the casserole in a larger baking pan, and pour in enough hot water to come halfway up the outer side of the casserole. Bake for 1 hour. When ready, a tester inserted 2 inches from the side should come out clean.

The center will appear underbaked, and the texture will be somewhere between cake and pudding. Cool.

To make the Chantilly cream, beat together the cream, sugar, and vanilla until softly whipped. The consistency should be a bit runny.

To serve, divide the pudding equally among 6 dessert plates and top with the cream and berries.

Yields 6 servings

Frozen Raspberry Mousse

A simply delicious summer treat!

> 3 cups fresh raspberries, rinsed and dried
> 1½ cups superfine sugar
> ¼ cup water
> 1½ teaspoons framboise
> 5 egg whites
> 2½ cups heavy cream

Using a blender, purée 2 cups of the raspberries, 1 cup of the sugar, the water, and framboise, for 3 minutes until smooth.

Beat the egg whites with an electric mixer until they hold soft peaks. Continuing to mix, gradually add the remaining sugar, until the egg whites become stiff and glossy, like a meringue.

Pour the raspberry purée into a large mixing bowl and spoon the egg whites on top.

Using the same bowl in which you beat the egg whites, whip the cream until it holds soft peaks. Spoon the whipped cream over the egg whites. With a rubber spatula, gently fold the mixture until it all turns a pretty pink and no white stripes remain. Spoon the mousse into a freezer-safe serving bowl, cover, and freeze.

Fifteen minutes before ready to serve, remove the mousse from the freezer. Spoon into individual dishes and top with remaining cup of raspberries.

Yields 6 to 8 servings

> ❄ As this contains raw eggs, you might not want to serve it to the very young, the very old, or anyone with a compromised immune system.

Frozen Orange Mousse

Serve alongside a brownie or top with fresh summer berries and a spoonful of Crème Fraîche (page 30). The mousse can be made up to a week ahead and stored, covered, in the freezer.

1 cup frozen orange juice concentrate

1½ cups superfine sugar

2 teaspoons Grand Marnier (optional)

Grated zest of 1 orange

4 egg whites

2 cups heavy cream

Fresh mint, for garnish

Place the frozen orange juice, 1¼ cups of the sugar, the Grand Marnier, and orange zest in a food processor fitted with a metal blade. Purée 3 minutes until smooth. Pour into a large bowl.

In a separate bowl, using an electric mixer, whip the egg whites. As soft peaks begin to hold, gradually add the remaining sugar while whipping, until the texture is stiff and glossy. Scoop onto the orange purée.

Using the same bowl in which you beat the egg whites, whisk the cream until soft peaks hold. Spoon over the the egg whites. With a rubber spatula, gently fold the mixture until it all turns golden yellow and no white stripes remain. Spoon the mousse into a freezer-safe dish, cover, and freeze until needed.

To serve, scoop portions into six to eight large wineglasses and top with mint sprigs.

Yields 6 to 8 servings

❦ As this contains raw eggs, you might not want to serve it to the very young, the very old, or anyone with a compromised immune system.

Frozen Chocolate–Mocha Mousse

This mousse has been a Loaves and Fishes runaway best seller for many years now. It can be kept in the freezer for weeks, scooped out as you would ice cream into a pretty bowl or glass, served with a crisp cookie on the side and presto: instant dessert!

5 ounces semisweet chocolate

½ cup hot strong brewed coffee

1 tablespoon Kahlúa

1¼ cups sugar

6 eggs, separated

2 cups heavy cream

Whipped cream, for garnish

Grated or shaved chocolate, for garnish

Mint leaves, for garnish

Using a food processor, finely grate the chocolate. Transfer to a large bowl. Pour the hot coffee over the chocolate and let stand for about 10 minutes until melted. Add the Kahlúa and stir to blend.

Using an electric stand mixer, beat 1 cup of the sugar and the egg yolks until light and fluffy. Add the melted chocolate to the egg mixture. Mix just to combine. Transfer to a large bowl.

Wash and dry the mixer bowl and beaters or whisk. Pour in the egg whites and whisk until soft peaks form. With the mixer running, slowly add the remaining ¼ cup sugar until the whites hold soft peaks. Spoon the egg whites onto the chocolate mixture.

Using the same bowl in which you beat the egg whites, whisk the cream until soft peaks form. Spoon the whipped cream over the egg whites. With a rubber spatula, gently fold the egg whites, whipped cream, and chocolate until

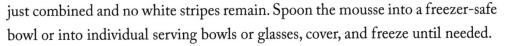

just combined and no white stripes remain. Spoon the mousse into a freezer-safe bowl or into individual serving bowls or glasses, cover, and freeze until needed.

Decorate the mousse with whipped cream, grated or shaved chocolate, and a sprig of mint.

Yields 6 to 8 servings

❧ There are other coffee-flavored liqueurs, but I like using Kahlúa.

❧ As this contains raw eggs, you might not want to serve it to the very young, the very old, or anyone with a compromised immune system.

Chocolate Brownies

There is nothing like a rich, dark fudge brownie in the middle of the afternoon with a cup of strong black coffee. This is heaven for chocolate lovers around the world.

3 ounces semisweet chocolate, cut into chunks

3 ounces unsweetened chocolate, cut into chunks

24 tablespoons (12 ounces) unsalted butter, cut into small cubes

6 large eggs

3 cups sugar

1½ teaspoons instant espresso powder

1 tablespoon vanilla extract

½ teaspoon kosher salt

1½ cups unbleached all-purpose flour

Preheat the oven to 350°F. Butter a 13 x 9-inch baking pan.

While the oven is heating, combine the chocolates and butter in an ovenproof bowl. Melt in the oven for about 8 to 10 minutes. Let cool for 30 minutes.

Whisk together the eggs, sugar, espresso, vanilla, and salt. Add to the chocolate-butter mixture and beat well to blend. Add the flour. Stir until the batter is smooth. Spread the batter evenly in the baking pan.

Bake 30 minutes. Cool completely in the pan. Cut into 24 bars.

Yields 24 brownies

❋ The uncut brownies, when covered and refrigerated, will keep up to 1 week. (If they last that long!)

Lemon Cookies with Dried Cherries

Try substituting any other dried fruit that you fancy. Diced dates taste really terrific, as does the humble raisin.

> 8 tablespoons (4 ounces) butter, softened
>
> 8 tablespoons (4 ounces) margarine, softened
>
> 1½ cups sugar
>
> 1½ teaspoons grated lemon zest
>
> 2 eggs
>
> 3½ cups unbleached all-purpose flour
>
> 2 teaspoons baking soda
>
> 2 cups dried cherries

Preheat the oven to 375°F.

With an electric mixer, cream the butter, margarine, and sugar for about 5 minutes, until light and fluffy. Add the lemon zest and eggs. Mix at low speed until well blended. Add the flour, baking soda, and dried cherries. Mix at low speed just to blend.

With your hands roll out 1-inch balls and place them 3 inches apart on 1 or 2 ungreased baking sheets. Dip a fork into cold water and flatten the cookies a little, making crisscross patterns on each top.

Bake 8 to 10 minutes, or until the edges are light brown. Remove from the oven and cool on the baking sheet.

Placed in an airtight container, the cookies will last a week.

Yields 50 cookies

Coconut-Oatmeal Cookies

Happiness is finding a full cookie jar when you come home from school, work, or play. Crunchy and sweet, these are bound to please the child in all of us.

2 cups unbleached all-purpose flour

1 cup sugar

1 teaspoon baking powder

1 teaspoon baking soda

½ teaspoon kosher salt

1 packed cup light brown sugar

16 tablespoons (8 ounces) unsalted butter, softened

2 large eggs

1 teaspoon vanilla extract

1½ cups rolled oats

1 cup chopped walnuts

1 cup sweetened shredded coconut

Granulated sugar, for dipping

Preheat the oven to 375°F. Butter a baking sheet.

Combine the flour, sugar, baking powder, baking soda, and salt in a mixer bowl. Add the brown sugar, butter, eggs, and vanilla. Beat at low speed to mix well. Add the oats, walnuts, and coconut. Stir to blend.

With your hands, roll the dough into balls about 1½ inches in diameter. Dip the tops in granulated sugar and place on the baking sheet 2 inches apart. Bake 12 to 14 minutes, or until lightly browned. Cool on the baking sheet.

Placed in an airtight container, the cookies will last up to a week.

Yields 30 to 35 cookies

Lemon Bars

If you enjoy a dessert both tangy and sweet, try these.

Crust

> 3½ cups unbleached all-purpose flour
>
> ¾ cup plus 2 tablespoons confectioners' sugar
>
> 16 tablespoons (8 ounces) unsalted butter, chilled and cut into small pieces
>
> 12 tablespoons (6 ounces) margarine, cut into small pieces

Filling

> 7 large eggs
>
> 3½ cups sugar
>
> ½ cup plus 1 tablespoon fresh lemon juice
>
> ⅔ cup unbleached all-purpose flour
>
> 1 teaspoon baking soda
>
> Confectioners' sugar, for dusting

Preheat the oven to 350°F.

With your hands, mix the flour, confectioners' sugar, butter, and margarine in a large bowl until crumbly. Press into the bottom of a 17 x 12-inch baking sheet with a 1-inch rim. Bake 15 minutes, or until the crust is baked through but not browned. Leave the oven on.

To make the filling, beat together the eggs, sugar, and lemon juice. Combine the flour and baking soda and add to the mixture. Beat to blend. Pour over the baked crust. Bake 25 minutes. Cool in the pan. Dust with confectioners' sugar before cutting.

Cover tightly with plastic wrap and store in the refrigerator up to a week.

Yields 20 bars

Metric Equivalencies

Liquid Equivalencies

Customary	Metric
¼ teaspoon	1.25 milliliters
½ teaspoon	2.5 milliliters
1 teaspoon	5 milliliters
1 tablespoon	15 milliliters
1 fluid ounce	30 milliliters
¼ cup	60 milliliters
⅓ cup	80 milliliters
½ cup	120 milliliters
1 cup	240 milliliters
1 pint (2 cups)	480 milliliters
1 quart (4 cups)	960 milliliters (.96 liter)
1 gallon (4 quarts)	3.84 liters

Dry Measure Equivalencies

Customary	Metric
1 ounce (by weight)	28 grams
¼ pound (4 ounces)	114 grams
1 pound (16 ounces)	454 grams
2.2 pounds	1 kilogram (1,000 grams)

Oven Temperature Equivalencies

Description	°Fahrenheit	°Celsius
Cool	200	90
Very slow	250	120
Slow	300–325	150–160
Moderately slow	325–350	160–180
Moderate	350–375	180–190
Moderately hot	375–400	190–200
Hot	400–450	200–230
Very hot	450–500	230–260

Index